How To Become A

JOURNALIST

The Insider's guide to getting a career in Journalism

Nick Rennie

Orders: Please contact Nick Rennie.

You can also order via the e mail address: nrennie157@gmail.com

ISBN: 978-0-9933928-0-1

First published 2015

Printed in Great Britain for Nick Rennie by Bell & Bain Ltd, 303 Burnfield Road, Thornliebank, Glasgow G46 7UQ

CONTENTS

INTRODUCTION

This book came about because I am constantly asked what it is like to be a journalist and how I managed to become one.

These questions are fired at me from schoolchildren, university students, young people who are undecided about what to do with their lives and people who are desperate for a career change.

I also get regularly asked by trainee journalists for tips on how they can do their job better.

The upshot of all this was that I started thinking there was a real need for a definitive book explaining exactly How To Become A Journalist.

The books that are out there on this subject appear to be quite dated with little consideration for the demands made on modern journalists since the rise of the internet and online journalism.

They are also a little formal with no regard for what it is like to actually be in the maelstrom of a busy newsroom.

I wanted to write a guide about the talents and personal qualities you need to do the job.

The book needed to explain what training there is available and how people can become a journalist without any relevant qualifications.

It had to include recent advances in digital journalism and why online news outlets have become almost more important than the printed newspaper or magazine.

There had to be a section on social media and how it acts as another channel to publish news and sport to your readership and its uses as a powerful tool for discovering news, often seconds after it has broken.

The book wouldn't be complete if I hadn't included basic advice on how to write stories – the building blocks you need to have in place to make your articles flow and attract someone to read them.

I've also addressed the crucial aspect of the news 'hook' – being able to identify immediately what is newsworthy about a potential story and how significant it is.

This is very much a book which takes the reader behind the scenes at a newspaper or magazine and into the mind of an insider who has been there and done it.

It is partly aimed at someone who is considering taking a journalism degree or NCTJ training.

But it is also written with those individuals in mind who want to go into the profession with no journalism qualifications behind them.

If you take everything on board you will be in a great position to not only gain an interview for a trainee journalism post but also to get offered the job.

And if you have already started working as a rookie reporter this book will enable you to develop your skills and advance more swiftly along the career path you want to take.

At this point I should explain a little about myself.

I have been a newspaper journalist for 27 years, working on local, regional and national newspapers during that time.

I've done virtually every job on a newspaper.

After starting as a trainee with no previous experience on the Melton Times in Leicestershire, I moved up the career ladder to a news editor's post at the Suffolk Free Press, where I managed a team of reporters and enjoyed the responsibility of setting the news agenda for the first time.

I then went on to become a sports writer at the daily Colchester Evening Gazette before taking my first sports editor's role at the Bucks Herald in Aylesbury.

After another sports editorship at one of the world's oldest newspapers, the Rutland and Stamford Mercury, I worked for a short period for a national newspaper in the Bahamas.

Since then I have been a district news reporter at the big-selling regional daily, the Leicester Mercury, and a sports editor and features editor at the countywide Rutland Times.

I've been a news freelance at various newspapers since then, working as a multi-media journalist, taking photographs as well as writing for online and print.

I've been lucky enough to win several awards for my news and sports writing and my all-round journalism.

And I've had the pleasure of passing on my experience and expertise to schoolchildren at careers days and to journalism degree students as a guest lecturer at university.

I still enjoy the job immensely and hopefully that passion will come through as we move through this book.

The principles I will outline hold true for any branch of journalism, whether your aim is to be a local newspaper reporter, a columnist for a national newspaper or an investigative reporter at CNN.

Many of our most celebrated journalists cut their teeth on small provincial newspapers and they will all pay tribute to the solid grounding this provided for them.

Finally, let me answer those questions posed at the start of this introductory chapter.

I managed to become a journalist completely by chance. I was a fitness instructor at the time after passing a sports science degree and envisaged a career in the leisure industry.

While serving in the bar one night I got chatting to some reporters from a local newspaper.

Their stories about life in the newsroom really fired my imagination but, of course, a career at that stage was no more than a pipe dream.

It set me thinking, though, because I had a love of English language and literature while at school.

When those reporters came in the bar the following week I mentioned my interest in re-training in their profession and, as luck would have it, one of them told me about a vacancy for a trainee reporter on one of their sister newspapers.

I applied for the job and to my surprise and total elation I was taken on as a rookie journalist.

I was mentored there by an experienced journalist called Lyndon Whittaker and his influence was invaluable in knocking off my rough edges in those early days.

And in answer to the other question: it is an extremely satisfying and rewarding job being a journalist.

You get a real buzz when you break a story, often of major importance to your community or even your country, and knowing that people heard it from you first.

The job allows you to meet people from all walks of life and motivates you to research and learn about issues and topics you might never otherwise have come across.

Being a journalist will often get you the best seat in the house at a theatre or a major sporting event.

You will get to meet your heroes and I have met many of mine.

Your notebook and pen will give you access to famous people and individuals with great influence in the world.

Sure there are some dull moments like any other job. Parish council meetings on a dark, wet Monday night spring to mind or sitting waiting for hours on end for cases to be heard at a court house.

But there is plenty to enjoy about being a journalist and I intend to convince you over the coming pages that it is the career for you.

Finally, I would like to thank Richard McMunn for being my mentor for this book.

Richard is a multiple best-selling author of non-fiction books with many of them helping hundreds of people get into a new career.

I'm confident mine will do just that too.

CHAPTER 1

NINE PERSONAL QUALITIES THAT YOU NEED TO BE A JOURNALIST

CHAPTER 1: Nine personal qualities that you need to be a journalist

When anyone considers applying for a vacancy or making a career change the first question they usually ask themselves is: Can I do this job?

It may be that they have already taken a training course or a university degree in preparation for a profession or, like I was, they are employed doing something totally unrelated.

That person might also be a sixth former considering their employment options for when they leave school.

Journalists come from all social and ethnic backgrounds. Some of them are university graduates or people who have taken a related training course but plenty have started out with no journalistic qualifications.

However, there are a specific set of personal qualities you need to make a success of the job.

It is not necessary to have all of the following but as long as you possess a good number of them then I would advise you to seriously consider making a career in journalism.

1. AN INQUIRING MIND

Journalists want to find things out and they like to challenge authority. They constantly seek authentic sources for stories to back-up a tip-off or a leak.

How many times do you hear people say 'don't believe what you read in a newspaper'?

In fact, newspapers and broadcasting outlets are some of the few remaining sources of news you can believe because they check facts.

In a world when anyone can publish their thoughts online with the click of a mouse we are awash with opinions on social media and internet forums, many of which are based on hearsay, which is defined as information received from other people which cannot be substantiated.

The job of a journalist is to publish the truth in a balanced way, with reference to both sides of an issue or argument.

Asking questions of trusted sources is the only way to achieve this.

Most organisations and businesses now have a communications team but their press releases are a sanitised version of their news, heavily biased with their own viewpoint.

Journalists go beyond the press release. They will ask additional questions and also go to another source to give an alternative view.

You need to be inquisitive to thrive in the world of journalism. That means having your eyes and ears open to potential news stories when you are driving to work, walking down the street or watching television.

2. GOOD GENERAL KNOWLEDGE

As a news and features writer you will be covering subjects you know nothing about and which you've never before had an interest in.

I remember as a cub reporter being sent out on one of my first assignments to interview a man about his taxidermy business, the art of preparing, stuffing and mounting the skins of dead animals.

Now, I knew next to nothing about this practice and this was before the age of the internet so I had no way of doing any research at short notice.

I had to rely on asking questions about every aspect of his work and, fortunately, he had sufficient passion about his work that he was happy to spoon-feed me the information.

These days we can always rely on Google to mug up on something in a few seconds.

But you will find yourself in situations where a story breaks around you or it assumes a different focus and so it is important to know about as wide a range of topics as possible.

Your mind needs to act like a sponge, soaking up information and intelligence when you are watching television, reading a newspaper or magazine or listening to the radio.

If you approach someone for an interview it helps if you know what you are talking about, even if it is just a working knowledge about something or someone.

This is particularly true when you are a young reporter when older people or senior members of an organisation might have doubts that you possess the necessary authority or gravitas to tell their story.

3. DEDICATION

It's a fact of modern life that many of us do a lot more hours at work than we are actually paid for, whatever job we do.

Journalism is certainly not a profession for someone who is a clock-watcher.

You'll be asked to cover evening meetings at your local council on a provincial weekly newspaper or you might have to stay in the office to reach an important source for a story who is unavailable during working hours.

Some news outlets operate a weekend rota system where reporters take turns to be on call on a Saturday and Sunday.

And, of course, if you are on the sports desk then you will likely be out reporting on matches at weekends.

The night before deadline day or 'press day' as it is often called, might involve a couple of extra hours in the office.

So you will work unsociable hours as a journalist. But in most cases you will be able to take time off in lieu to soften the blow of missing a family event or a night at the cinema with your partner.

The need to update websites 24/7 means today's journalists are more and more likely to be working late but it's a small price we pay for reporting the news efficiently and as quickly as possible.

There was a time when weekly reporters had plenty of down time with deadlines often days away. But every newspaper has a website now and multiple social media channels so every journalist is effectively working for a daily, real time, news agency.

4. AN ATTENTION TO DETAIL

I once spelled someone's name wrong in a feature I was writing about a blind man who was running his own successful printing business.

In fact, both his first name and his surname were incorrectly spelt. I was a young reporter at the time and didn't initially feel it was a major error.

That was until the man called and said he didn't recognise the person in the story because his name wasn't right.

The editor decided to run the story again with the name spelled correctly and a new photo to give it some semblance of freshness.

It was an important lesson for me and ever since I have checked names rigorously.

If someone is called John check if his name is spelled Jon and if his surname is Smith make sure it isn't spelled Smyth.

Accuracy is everything. Never assume anything. Fact checking is one of the proud boasts of journalists the world over.

It is what distinguishes us from bloggers and those who break news on social media sites, often via someone who they thought was telling them the truth.

Journalists also work within the law, mainly because we can be sued for libelling someone, but also because it protects the integrity of what we do.

How many times have you seen a Tweet or a Facebook post where the writer clearly has no grasp of the facts and is often motivated by personal beliefs and prejudices.

A recent survey found that local newspapers and news broadcasters were the most trusted sources of news, with three times as many people citing these outlets compared to those who trusted Facebook posts and comments.

And this is purely down to the fact that journalists check facts.

5. A THICK SKIN

If you can't take criticism then journalism is not the career for you.

You will get occasional abuse via a telephone caller who is unhappy you didn't cover their story in the latest issue.

Members of the public might have a go at you at a community meeting about something the paper printed – it might not even have been your article but you will have to sit and take it.

And there can be threats and verbals aimed at you while you are covering court cases or attending sensitive hearings such as inquests.

There will also be occasions when you attend distressing events, like funerals or memorial services for people who have died in tragic circumstances.

You might feel you are intruding in some cases but you maintain an air of professionalism because these occasions are in the public interest.

I recall attending the funeral of a 12-year-old boy who was knocked off his bike and killed while delivering newspapers.

It was an upsetting experience just listening to the service but having to make notes as well with the child's grieving relatives and friends around me was quite a challenge.

One of the boy's uncles made a point of seeking me out as I left the church and thanked me for taking the trouble to attend and write a tribute piece about his nephew.

There'll be other times when your stomach is turned by evidence given at a violent murder trial or an animal cruelty case.

Or you might be asked to interview members of the local foxhunting group when you abhor the sport.

But in all of these cases you are there to report the news, fairly and accurately and you can't let the subject matter get to you.

6. TRUSTFULNESS

Nailing good stories is often about getting people to trust you, either in the way you approach them or how you deal with them over a period of time.

So you need to be good with people to be a journalist and be able to build relationships with key influencers in the community or the industry you cover.

Having good contacts is essential because they will lead to a steady flow of stories and when something big breaks they might give you that all important tip-off or access to someone who will tell you the information.

The first step is keeping an up-to-date contacts book and staying in touch with key people in it.

You'll occasionally be told information 'off the record' to give you background to a report you are working on.

There will be a big temptation to use these nuggets when they would give you a big exclusive.

But if you've agreed to respect the 'off the record' convention with your source then you are duty bound not to act on the information.

This is another element of trust which contacts will value and they will keep coming back to you with potential stories in the future.

You'll also come across confidential or sensitive information which should not be used in a newspaper article or on a radio bulletin.

This is particularly true in local weekly titles although tabloid newspapers routinely trample over these conventions, of course.

For example, you might learn that the local Mayor has cancelled engagements after being diagnosed with a potentially life-threatening illness.

As a journalist you need to respect the privacy of an individual, particularly when some members of their family or their friends are unaware of the situation.

Similarly, if you have learned the identity of a victim in a road accident shortly after it happened you should not reveal their identity until a formal press release has been issued by the police.

7. TACTFULNESS

There are many occasions when journalists are required to show tact and understanding.

From early in your career, you will be asked to interview family members of people killed in tragic accidents.

Clearly, this is often a difficult task even for the most seasoned of journalists.

But if you are someone who typically treats others with respect then you will find it more comfortable.

The sole aim of this kind of story is to produce an article which acts as a tribute to the person who has died.

You are not looking to unearth murky family secrets or suspicious activity from their past but instead you are aiming to record that person's life history and reflect how important they were to their family and to the community they lived in.

There will be occasions when people you are interviewing will be emotional and sometimes tearful so you need to be aware of how your questions are affecting them and stop if they are obviously upset.

You might be surprised by the reaction of some bereaved relatives. They may laugh about memories of the person who has passed away or they could appear unnervingly cheerful.

This is a natural human reaction by some who use it as a coping mechanism.

It's also important to realise that some people will welcome you into their home because they are desperate to talk about a loved one.

This is because friends or neighbours, perhaps, have avoided talking about the person who has passed away for fear of offending them.

So showing respect for people is an important quality in a journalist.

And this also extends to those you don't like because of what they have done or due to the organisation they represent.

Always remember that you are an ambassador for the news outlet you work for. And that means reflecting all views on an issue even if you find them reprehensible or ridiculous.

8. IMPARTIALITY

If you eventually progress to a national newspaper you might be required to write articles with a political slant.

But when you're starting out you can't reveal any leaning towards a political party.

The same goes for religion. Your own personal thoughts should not intrude on the stories you file.

If they do you will swiftly be taken to task by your editor.

This is particularly the case at election time when you are required to reflect the views of candidates for local councils and for parliamentary office.

In fact, there is legislation in place in the run-up to elections which dictates that coverage must reflect the range of political views in the community.

There will be issues you have strong views about but you can't let these impinge on your reporting.

You might hate foxhunting, for example, but you should always look to represent the views of local hunters as well as the saboteurs or the anti-hunt lobby.

Think of yourself as the host in a public debate. You should aim to let everyone have their say equally while putting the discussion in context for the audience (readers).

Another aspect where you need to remain neutral is where you are writing about businesses.

Even though you might be one of the most loyal customers of a local café you shouldn't be promoting how good they are or what great value their all-day breakfast is.

By the same token, if a local tradesman has given you shoddy service this should not be reflected in your articles.

There will be occasions when you get offered an opportunity to review a restaurant.

Now, you will doubtless be very grateful to have been served three courses on the house but your review should reflect the experience you had.

It's a different situation, of course, if it is a paid-for advertorial where the business has paid for the space in your newspaper, but if this is purely an editorial review then your report should be objective and unbiased.

If you have strong opinions on politics, religion or important issues then there will still be journalistic openings for you, in newspapers and magazines which reflect similar viewpoints to you.

But as a journalist starting out your aim is to be impartial in everything you write and to produce copy which respects multiple perspectives.

9. SENSE OF HUMOUR

Lastly, and some journalists might say, most importantly, is the requirement to have a laugh in the job.

This doesn't mean having a joke at the expense of colleagues, although this sometimes happens.

But it is more to do with enjoying the job for what it is. You will come across some characters and news items which are genuinely hilarious.

And the atmosphere in a newsroom can often be lively and full of humour.

You might have to put up with colleagues who suddenly engage in a punathon, riffing words associated with the headline of an offbeat story.

Or there might be a brainstorm on potential erroneous articles to mark April Fool's Day or the subject matter for the weekly cartoon based around a news item from that week.

There is also a fair measure of black humour in the wake of a depressingly bleak story.

Like those who work in the emergency services, journalists often get close to the main players in a tragedy and sometimes the only way for some to cope is to make light of it.

Not everyone in the newsroom will react like that, of course, but it can happen.

A sense of humour is important in most office-bound jobs and journalism is no different.

Now that we understand the qualities required to become a journalist, we can start to explore some of the more important techniques journalists use to create fantastic stories.

In the next chapter I will explain how to find the hook in any news story.

The tips and advice I am going to teach you will enable you to create fascinating and high impact news stories and articles which, in turn, will make you a great journalist!

CHAPTER 2

FINDING THE HOOK IN A NEWS STORY AND HOW TO INTERVIEW

CHAPTER 2: Finding the hook in a news story and how to interview

FINDING THE 'HOOK' IN A NEWS STORY

If there is one outstanding thing you should aim to learn from this book it is the ability to identify what makes a news story.

Journalists often call it spotting the 'hook', that special ingredient which you hang your story on.

It's a skill which is unfortunately lost on many who work in public relations.

I have seen countless press releases during my career which are nothing more than a promotional piece for a company or organisation.

There is no story value to this content from a journalism perspective – it is better off pitched as advertising copy.

If you were able to cut through a good news story, like a stick of rock, most, or all, of the following specific features would be in all of them:

- **It's new** (you are reporting it for the first time or you have found a different angle on a story which has already broken and, in both cases, it has just happened)

- **It's important** (the event or issue you are reporting has a significance)

- **It's relevant to your readers, listeners or viewers** (the story impacts on their lives or the lives of their relatives, friends or peers)

- **There is a human interest angle** (a person or persons is/are involved in, or affected by, your story)

At this point I want to set you a little test – to find out what kind of news sense you possess. Don't worry if you find it difficult at this stage. Many aspiring and trainee journalists struggle at first to find the hook in a story.

I want you to imagine you are sitting at your desk in a newsroom and the following fictitious emails have come in asking you to report on them for your newspaper or broadcaster.

There is a news story buried in all of them and your task is to identify that all-important 'hook' and then write down in a few sentences why.

A little trick which might help here is to imagine you are telling your mum and dad or a friend about it. What would you tell them?

Email 1

Dear Nick

I am the District Scout Leader for Oxdown and we are holding a recruitment day for people interested in becoming Scout leaders with the packs in our area.

We have got quite a few leaders signed up anyway but we always organise a recruitment day every year to give those who are interested the chance to find out more about what we do.

The event is at Scout HQ, in Travis Avenue, at 2pm this coming Saturday.

We've been running for exactly 50 years in the town and we've got more Scouts than we've ever had.

If you could publicise our recruitment day that would be great.

Regards,

Chris Smith

Email 2

Dear Nick

Apologies for the delay in sending you this email about the changes to the line-up for the village fete this weekend.

My neighbour had a baby yesterday and I got involved helping with that.

Anyway, the marching band will now be on at 3pm and not 2pm as I said before.,

We've also got a new act lined up, a motorcycle display team who jump through hoops of fire.

That should be really popular.

The charity for this year, if I've not mentioned it before, is the local hospice.

If you need any more call me at home later. If I'm not here my husband will be. He might be sleeping though because he had to deliver my neighbour's baby in his car last night while they were going to hospital, bless him.

If you can send a photographer to the fete at 2.30pm, the Mayor should be around to pose in a photograph.

Best wishes,

Jane Johnson

Email 3

Dear Nick

Our parish council meeting was held last night and we decided to object to that planning application in Midas Street where the owner wants to extend his property and build a granny flat in the back garden.

All the neighbours down there are up in arms about it.

By the way, thanks for the report you did last week on the front page about people spotting that panther in the village.

We all bought a copy and we've had a good laugh about it to be honest.

One of the farmers reckons he got a photograph of the panther – he says he's never seen an animal that big in the wild before.

So there must be something in it.

Anyway I will let you know if we spot it again.

I can send you the minutes of the parish meeting if that helps you with that planning story.

Regards,

Stan Topham

Now let's look in detail at the news hook in each story and I will explain exactly why you should base your article around it.

Email 1

This is a classic example of the real story being buried in an otherwise mundane email.

Chris has emailed me specifically to ask me to publicise his Scout leader recruitment event, even though he admits they are not short of leaders and it is something they do every year.

It is the line *We've been running for exactly 50 years in the town and we've got more Scouts than we've ever had* which is the real story here.

You will need to go back to Chris and get some information about the history of the Scouts or find an alternative source with that information.

If we refer back to those four key components of a news story I mentioned earlier in the chapter we can see why the anniversary is the hook:

- **It's new** – the 50th anniversary has just been reached

- **It's important** – half-a-century is significant for any organisation

- **It's relevant to our audience** – some readers will have been involved with the Scouts in your patch and many will have children who were Scouts

- **Human interest angle** – as above, and there is also the line that it is very popular among local children

The red herring in this email was the Scout leader recruitment event – you could mention it at the end of your story but the revelation that the organisation is 50 years old lends itself to a historical piece with pictures of Scout groups going back through the years if you can get hold of them.

Email 2

This email is predominantly about the upcoming village fete and changes to the schedule.

But, again, the real story is about the baby and, specifically, Jane's husband delivering the neighbour's baby in his car while en route to the hospital.

It's clear that Jane doesn't even think the baby's birth is newsworthy so it will be a case of going back to her and asking if you can speak to her husband and the baby's mum and ideally get a picture of them both down at the hospital with the newborn.

Let's take a look at why this is the angle you should pursue:

- **It's new** – the event happened last night

- **It's important** – it is dramatic and unusual for a baby to be delivered outside a hospital or a home by someone who is not a member of the family

- **It's relevant to our audience** – both families live locally and they will be known to other readers, listeners or viewers

- **Human interest angle** – the incident is a real human drama significantly affecting people's lives

It's a fair chance your news outlet will be doing an article about the fete and the information about the acts and the charity can be added to that piece or included in the 'what's on' section if it is being covered there.

Email 3

This one is probably the most difficult one to identify the main story angle for someone with little or no journalistic experience.

The planning row is a potential story in its own right but it is relevant to only a small number of people, namely the householder who has made the application and the neighbours. It is a small development as well so it has limited appeal in terms of a major news story.

Experienced journalists will have honed in on the line *One of the farmers reckons he got a photograph of the panther – he says he's never seen an animal that big in the wild before.*

This is why you should identify this as the 'hook'.

- **It's new** – your newspaper covered the story the previous week but the story has moved on because there is now a photograph and evidence the panther actually exists

- **It's important** – villagers need to be aware there is a large wild cat prowling around

- **It's relevant to our audience** – the village is in your patch and there is a possibility the panther could roam into neighbouring villages and towns

- **Human interest angle** – Stan said there had been some laughter about the story but there will be fear now among some residents that there is evidence the animal is at large

You may get two stories out of this email because you could also argue that the planning story is new (the parish council is objecting), it's important (for people living in that particular road), it's relevant (the village is in your patch) and there is a human interest angle (neighbours are upset their quality of life would be spoiled by the development).

The main story is the panther, though. Your title reported it on the front page the previous week and it is a sufficiently unusual and interesting event to have a potentially dangerous wild animal on the prowl that you should go big on it again, as long as you can get hold of that farmer's photograph, of course.

Hopefully, you've now got a good grasp of what makes a news story. In the second part of this chapter I will explain how you should go about interviewing someone, whether you have a notebook in your hand, a radio microphone or a television camera.

This is a difficult skill for some to master, particularly if you are introverted or not overly self-confident. If you follow the advice I give you here it will make the whole process a lot easier.

And, in any case, you will be surprised the confidence you derive in an interview situation from having a notepad or a microphone.

I have interviewed some very famous people in my career, such as the then Prime Minister Tony Blair in 1998. I've also conducted interviews with some of my sporting heroes, like footballer Geoff Hurst and cricketer Brian Lara. In each of these situations I would have been extremely nervous to meet them in a different context but to interview them in an official capacity for my newspaper I felt empowered, confident and in total control of the situation.

Interviewing is something you can only really improve with practice. And then more practice. Here are some pointers which will put you at your ease and help you get the information you require for your report.

19 TOP TIPS ON HOW TO CONDUCT AN INTERVIEW FOR THE MEDIA

- ## 1 Prepare well

Make sure you mug up on the person you are about to interview and the issue you are reporting on. Check through back copies of your newspaper or previous broadcasts and do an online search for any related stories which are relevant. It helps when you are a trainee to list the important questions before the interview. But be prepared to ask other questions if the interview moves off in a different direction and a new angle emerges for your story. Your subject is likely to be more responsive if you are informed about them or the issue you are talking about so it is vitally important that you put in the preparation work.

- ## 2 Gauge how long the interview will be

Always ask at the start how long your subject has for the interview. Otherwise you may well be cut off before you've asked those all-important key questions. If you are pushed for time you need to ask the critical stuff right from the beginning. Make sure you have that information in your notebook. If the subject is short for time you could always try re-arranging the interview for a different time when they can spend more time with you, assuming that deadline is not fast approaching, of course.

- ## 3 Adopt the right tone

There will be times when you have to interview family members of someone who has died tragically. Clearly, you need to adopt a caring, sombre, respectful tone here and you should avoid any questions which are likely to upset or distress your subject. Other articles can be offbeat and humorous and in this instance there is nothing wrong with adopting a more light-hearted air to your questioning, while retaining a degree of professionalism. There can also be a different tone depending on how the interview is being conducted. If it is on the telephone and you have never met the individual before it is as well to introduce yourself and explain why you would like to do the report. When you interview someone in person it is easier to build that sense of trust just from being face-to-face with them.

• 4 Put the interviewee at their ease

On occasions you will interview someone who isn't used to talking to members of the press.

They will come across nervous and defensive and make your job that little bit more difficult.

If I am at someone's house I will make a point of bringing up something personal to the interviewee such as their pet dog or a nice painting on the wall. It's amazing how easily people will then relax even when they are talking about a sensitive subject. If your host offers you a cup of tea or coffee then accept it, even if you don't want one, because it will help you build a rapport with that person. If they offer you food, that's a different matter. I can remember interviewing an elderly couple about their diamond wedding celebrations. The wife offered me this lovely big cream cake which I proceeded to drip down my trousers, completely throwing me off my stride!

• 5 Listen to your subject

This might sound obvious. But you would be amazed how many journalists don't listen to what their subject is telling them. The end result, of course, is they get the story wrong and a complaint is invariably filed with the editor after it is published. When you are a trainee it is easy to furiously write everything down because you are desperate not to miss anything which is said. You are better advised just to sit there at the start and talk to the person in a normal conversation. And just write down the important stuff and information you are likely to use. If you miss something, for whatever reason, or you are not sure about it, then ask the person to go over it again. They want you to get the story right every bit as much as you do.

• 6 Keep the interview flowing

Most people like to talk about themselves and if you ask the right questions you will get a continuous flow of great answers. Inevitably, some will talk too much and others will barely give you anything back. Children are notoriously difficult to interview because they are often shy and just go blank when a newspaper or radio reporter asks them a question. Usually if you ask them how they feel about a certain issue or situation they will give you a good answer. A good phrase to ask people if they are recounting events in a chronological order is *'what happened next?'* You will see solicitors and barristers using it in court cases to keep a narrative going for the benefit of a jury or a judge.

• 7 Prevent the subject going off on a tangent

I can remember as a young reporter asking an elderly man about his experiences serving in the war for a memory lane feature. It was one of the most frustrating experiences I can remember as a journalist because he constantly went off on a different point to the one I had asked him about. He was also hard of hearing so my occasional interjections literally fell on deaf ears. The interview lasted a couple of hours when 30 minutes would have sufficed. The point is that as a young reporter I didn't have the confidence to intervene each time and eventually gave up on getting him to stick to the point. Something I have learned since then with interviews like this is to stop someone in mid-sentence and say *'I'm sorry but I only have 10 minutes left for the interview because I have another appointment'*. You will be surprised how quickly that focuses the mind and you get only the answers to the questions you are interested in.

• 8 Avoid asking closed questions

Avoid at all costs any questions where you are likely to get a *yes* or a *no* answer. You are giving the interviewee no leeway with their answers and you won't get the good quotes you are after. Questions like *'that was great wasn't it?'*, *'Did you enjoy that?'* or' *'Is that why you did that?'* are examples of this. It is one of the problems with interviewing children. There is no conversation element, invariably, so journalists will often lapse into asking questions aimed at reaffirming what the child is thinking and consequently they don't end up with any usable quotes in their notebooks. I can remember working as a sports writer and asking a depressed football manager straight after the match about his star striker's broken leg. He clearly didn't want to talk to me and just gave one word answers to every question. When I reflected on it later I realised I had asked too many closed questions and that was the real reason the interview failed.

• 9 Be tactful at all times

Never lose sight of the fact that the person you are interviewing is a real person. They have feelings and what you are talking to them about might have had an important impact on their life. Put yourself in their shoes. How would you like to be treated if a journalist was interviewing you? If someone becomes emotional or tearful when you are interviewing them then stop and give them a moment to compose themselves. Move the conversation onto something less sensitive. You can always return to the question which upset them if they are up to answering it later on. If a relative of your subject has died in an accident or of a serious illness you don't have to delve deeply into the details of it all. A relative is often keen to talk about the life of a loved one who has passed away suddenly but not the circumstances of their death.

• 10 Induce good quotes

The art of getting a good quote is a skill you can quickly learn. The aim is to get someone to open up and tell you in their own words about a dramatic or significant event, for example. Ask questions like *'how did you feel when that happened?'*, *'What sort of emotions were you going through at the time?'* or *'what do you think about that?'* will all get you great quotes. These are all examples of open questions, the total opposite of those closed questions we touched on earlier in this section. You know when you have a great quote. It hits you right between the eyes. I always put an asterisk next to a good quote so I can quickly find it in my notes when I come to write the story up.

• 11 Don't ask leading questions

There can often be a great temptation to put words in a person's mouth when you are interviewing them in an attempt to dramatise your report. For example, imagine you are interviewing witnesses to a huge fire or someone who has escaped a major accident. You might be tempted to say *'that must have been terrifying'* or *'it looked like you could have been killed in there'*. But don't say that to them. You want them to say *'I was terrified'* or *'I thought I was going to die'* and by phrasing the question differently you can achieve that. Better questions to have asked were *'what was it like being in that situation?'* and *'what sort of fears did you have being caught up in that?'*. You will then get quotes which will invariably be dramatic and all the more powerful because they came out unprompted. If you ask leading questions you aren't reporting the story accurately. By effectively telling someone how they felt in a situation you may well be getting a false impression of what went on. Barristers are prevented from asking leading questions of witnesses for precisely this reason.

• 12 Keep control

As a young reporter you may well still be learning shorthand and as a consequence you may struggle to keep up when you are taking notes in an interview. People talk at different speeds and even after you have passed the obligatory 100 words a minute shorthand test there will be occasions when you still can't get everything down because the interviewee or the speaker is talking too fast. In an interview situation there are little tricks you can use to slow down your subject. Interject with the odd question you don't really need the answer for, for example. While they are then addressing that point you ensure you have made a note of what they were previously talking about. I have also occasionally asked for a glass of water when I was desperate to finish off a note so I was able to then check I had it down accurately while they were out of the room. If you don't feel you have a clean note of it you can always then ask them to go over it again. It's a little trickier if you are in a press conference, a meeting or a public talk because you can't get the speaker to slow down. It's a good idea to take a digital recording device along in these instances or just concentrate on the very important passages and ensure you have a good note of those.

• 13 If you don't understand something, ask

There will be assignments where you don't know much about the subject or issue you are reporting on. It might be something highly technical or academic or a topic you just don't have a great knowledge of and haven't had a chance to research. But don't be afraid to ask the interviewee to explain something more simply. Your job as a newspaper or broadcast reporter is to report the story in a manner which makes it easy to understand for your audience. That is the skill of a journalist, to relate an issue or event in the simplest possible terms, to cut out the jargon and industry speak so the ordinary man or woman in the street can easily comprehend it.

• 14 Ensure you have everything ie 'the 5 Ws' who, what, where, why, when

One of the early things senior journalists drummed into me on my first newspaper was to remember 'the five Ws'. The *who, what, where, why, when* of a story. Basically, if you have the answer to these questions you have the basis for your story. When you are coming to the end of an interview for an article as an aspiring journalist or a trainee try to make a mental note of this or jot it down if you have the opportunity, perhaps when the photographer is organising his picture. If you have those answers then you have what you came for, assuming you have some killer quotes as well.

• 15 Ask challenging questions at the end

I remember interviewing a well-known married MP who had been on the national front pages at the time for having a secret child with a woman he had been having an affair with for several years. I had arranged the interview on the pretext of writing a feature about his career as an MP and what his job entailed. But the scandal he was involved in would obviously be the most interesting thing for our readers. So I went through my questions for the feature and then right at the end, when I was preparing to leave, I threw in one about the affair and the baby. He was reluctant to talk about it at first and got quite aggressive but eventually he opened up and told me about how he regularly saw his child and paid maintenance for her. It made a nice piece and came across more sympathetic than the reports in the big dailies. But had I asked the question about the affair right at the start of the interview I may well not have got to ask him any more questions. So the timing of your questions is important. Get down some notes initially so you have enough for your report and ask any sensitive questions near the end of the interview.

• 16 Standard final question

If you've followed the advice so far in this section you should already have enough information to put together a great story. But there may well be something you've forgotten to ask or that the interviewee would like to bring up. So always, always end your interview with the simple question *'is there anything else you would like to mention?'* You would be amazed how many times this yields golden nuggets for your piece. People often relax at this point as well because they know the interview has effectively finished so it can make them tell you something they might otherwise have kept to themselves. It's a trick Peter Falk used in that lovely old *Columbo* television detective series. After interviewing someone he leaves the room only to swiftly return and ask the suspect *'there's just one more thing'*. You are not trying to catch someone out but by asking them if they want to tell you anything else it occasionally gives you great additional content for your report and sometimes a completely new angle.

• 17 Organise a photo or ask to take one

On many occasions you will be conducting an interview in tandem with a photographer. But reporters are being tasked more and more to take their own photos, either with an office camera or on their mobile phone. It's always a good idea to ask to take a picture at the end of the interview, after you have gained their trust. Some people will still refuse because they don't want to be identified or they just value their own privacy. Radio reporters are also asked to take photos for use on their websites and if it is a celebrity interviewee they often take 'selfies'. If you've been asked to organise a photo by your editor for a later date make sure you take down contact details and the address and give the people you are interviewing plenty of options for times and dates, assuming you are not up against deadline.

• 18 Check spellings

It's a good idea to check your spellings at the end of an interview. It's important in every report you do as a journalist, of course, but when you are face to face with someone you have the opportunity to check you have it correct. Don't assume a name is spelled a certain way and don't ask if their name is spelled 'the usual way'. Even Smith can be Smyth, Smit or Smithe so get them to spell it out for you.

• 19 Take a contact number

This is particularly important if you are talking to someone you have interviewed by chance, a witness to a major event, for example, or someone who has called your news organisation to tell you something newsworthy. Even if the individual does not want to be named or identified in your report ask them for a telephone number – preferably a mobile so you can get them at any time of the day – in case you need to check something with them later. I can remember several occasions as a trainee journalist when I forgot to take contact details for someone and as a consequence I couldn't check anything with them and I missed out on getting a good photograph of them to go with my story.

You should now have a much greater understanding of what makes a news story and of the mechanics of how you interview someone and go about getting the information to create top notch reports.

In the next chapter I will take you through the technical aspects of actually writing a story, how you construct it and how you produce great copy. I will also talk about the art of headline writing so you can effectively draw the reader's eye to your stories.

CHAPTER 3

THE BUILDING BLOCKS OF A STORY AND HEADLINE WRITING

CHAPTER 3: The building blocks of a story and headline writing

So you've done your interview and you have all the important information in your notebook with good quotes and it is time to write up your report.

This is the tough part for trainees, actually putting together the story to get readers, listeners and viewers interested in it.

I can remember my early days in a newspaper office and the frustration I felt when the news editor tore my articles to pieces and totally re-wrote them.

In most cases I had all the details in my book but I wasn't able to articulate them in the way a journalist would do.

A bit like the old Eric Morecambe joke about a bad piano player – he plays all the right notes but not necessarily in the right order!

What I could have done with at the time was a template to work from – a structured framework to help me put each component of the story in the correct place.

So when I had the idea to write this book this was one of the key elements I wanted to include.

This is not an attempt to turn you into a robotic journalist but merely to help drum the principles into you.

Eventually the structure of a story will become second nature to you. By practising with the formula I give you later in this chapter the process will be a lot less painful than it was for me and fellow trainees of my generation.

KEY ELEMENTS OF A STORY

1 Introduction

This is undoubtedly the most crucial part of any story because if you don't grab the audience here they won't be interested in the rest of your piece.

Ask yourself what the story is and why it is important. Imagine you are telling someone about it. How would you phrase it? What details would you tell them first?

The intro should include dynamic words and a statement which announces that something significant is happening or has happened.

It also has to have a human element to it – was it an elderly person or a brave mum involved or did the story concern householders, schoolchildren or taxi drivers, for example.

You need to stress that it is new and avoid, at all costs, dating the story by including the phrases *last week* or *last month* or, worst of all, *recently*.

Tell the story as tightly as you can in that opening couple of lines and avoid jargon and over-complicated words so you don't instantly alienate some of your readers.

Avoid the temptation to over-dramatise your piece in a bid to wow the audience – stick to the facts but tell them in the most compelling way you can.

Examples of a good intro would be:

A brave Oxford pensioner has described how he fought off a mugger in one of the city's main car parks this morning.

Tube train drivers have decided to organise three periods of strike action in protest at plans to operate 24-hour services on the London Underground.

A passing lorry driver who raised the alarm after a house caught fire with a family of four asleep inside has been praised for his actions by firefighters.

2 Supporting phase

Now you need to keep the attention of your audience by adding supplementary information to back-up what you hit them with in the intro.

This is where you might refer more specifically to the location of an incident or the name of the individual or organisation involved.

These lines contain solid details which legitimise why the story is important and they will also include a great quote or two.

Someone might be telling you they are celebrating a great achievement, perhaps, or the survivor of a major accident will be explaining their emotions.

Here is how you might add to the examples of three intros from above:

A brave Oxford pensioner has described how he fought off a mugger in one of the city's main car parks this morning.

Gerald Mortimer (71) was arriving back at his car after a shopping trip when a man with a balaclava on suddenly grabbed him from behind and tried to take his carrier bags.

But the assailant ran off along the canal tow path after Mr Mortimer pushed him away.

The brave pensioner, who lives in Lyle Crescent, said: "I didn't have time to think. I wasn't going to let him take my shopping so I just pushed him off. He swore and then ran away."

Tube train drivers have decided to organise three periods of strike action in protest at plans to operate 24-hour services on the London Underground.

Drivers say they are unhappy they will be made to work through the night on some shifts despite being promised they wouldn't be.

A spokesperson for ASLEF, the train drivers' union, said: "Our members have no option but to strike on three days next month.

"They were told that they would not be made to work night shifts but the management have gone back on their promises."

A passing lorry driver who raised the alarm after a house caught fire with a family of four asleep inside has been praised for his actions by firefighters.

Paul Slocombe, who was en route to making a delivery at a supermarket in Leicestershire, saw flames coming from the house as he drove along Mycroft Way in Bogtown.

He stopped and banged on the front door to alert a couple and their two young children, who managed to escape from the property unhurt.

Gary Shelton, the incident commander who attended the scene with two fire engines from the city, said: "It was pure luck that Mr Slocombe was driving past the house at the time because the fire had taken hold in the roof by then.

"He acted very quickly to raise the alarm and thank goodness he did because we might have had a tragedy here if he hadn't."

3 Body

Once you've got sections 1 and 2 in place you need to make the rest of the story flow. You should aim to explain here how something happened and why it happened.

If it is a major incident you are reporting on, where people have been killed or injured, there will be a chronological order to what you write here.

For most lead stories you should try to gather quotes from at least two different sources, preferably with contrasting takes on your subject matter.

Their comments will then be weaved into your narrative to back up your account of the story.

We will look at how you go about writing the main body of the story shortly.

4 Concluding section

To finish your piece off you would generally include a quote from someone, perhaps reflecting on the issue or occurrence or predicting what is likely to happen in the future as a consequence.

When the story is about an individual or an organisation which is appealing for help in some way you would add relevant telephone, email or website details at the bottom of your story.

This is also the case with crime stories where the police are appealing for witnesses and they give out a phone line for people to contact.

If a story is being published with some kind of outcome hanging in the balance, you might add the phrase *'at the time of going to press'* in the event that the story quickly moves on.

STORY WRITING EXERCISES

The best way to learn how to write like a journalist is to practice so I will now set you three writing exercises.

I will provide sets of notes for fictitious stories and your task is to write articles using the four essential components I have outlined above.

You can then compare your efforts with reports I have written using the same notes.

Exercise 1: Notes from a telephone interview with a wheelchair-bound woman who painted her own disabled parking spot outside a school so she could safely deliver and pick-up her daughter.

Sophie Grant (32), Letsby Avenue, Stircaster.
Daughter Amy (5).
Stircaster Primary School on Todderton Rise, Stircaster.

"I was dropping off Amy on her first day of term and I couldn't find anywhere to park.
"The whole road was full of cars the other parents had parked there.
"It was so frustrating because I had to drive around for 20 minutes. In the end I had to wait for some of the others to drive off and Amy was late getting in to school."

Sophie had asked county council for a disabled parking spot outside the school and they said they would provide one.
She wrote to them in April and got a letter back in May saying she could have one.

Went back on Monday night and used spray paint to mark a space outside the school.
A couple of people came out to see what she was doing – they didn't object when she explained.

"It made me so angry because the council knew I needed that space.

"I have to park near the school and then get my wheelchair out so I can safely take Amy to school.

"She's a little girl and I don't want to have to walk her miles to get to school every morning."

Sophie has been disabled since a car accident three years ago. She drives an adapted car and can take her wheelchair to get in and out. Paralysed from the chest down.

"Since I became reliant on using a wheelchair I have been amazed how many issues disabled people have to deal with.

She went to B&Q to pick up spray paint – a local stationery shop gave her some stencils to spray the space evenly.

"Amy chose a nice bright pink colour in B&Q and I went back to the school in the evening and sprayed a nice big parking space for myself.

"It felt really good to be doing something positive about the situation.

"No-one parked in it this morning so I was able to stop outside the school and drop Amy off like all the other parents."

Sophie is not aware if she has committed a criminal offence. She has no regrets about doing it.

Stirton County Council statement:

We are very sorry about the trouble this matter has caused for Sophie and Amy.

We were intending to paint on the disabled space in time for the start of the term but this wasn't done.

The council would like to apologise for the inconvenience caused and we guarantee we will paint the parking bay in by the end of this week.

Tony Parmintor, head teacher of Stircaster Primary School:

Had spoken to Sophie in April about the possibility of having a disabled parking bay outside school.

Was happy for her to have one. Surprised it hadn't been painted on in time.

"I can totally understand Mrs Grant's frustration over this. She clearly needs to be able to park near to the school to drop Amy off and collect her safely.

"I have contacted the council on her behalf in a bid to get this done as soon as possible."

Mr Parmintor said this was the first request he had seen for a disabled parking space outside a school in the 20 years he has worked in education.

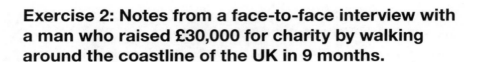

Exercise 2: Notes from a face-to-face interview with a man who raised £30,000 for charity by walking around the coastline of the UK in 9 months.

Bradley Stoker (51), Pinkerton Close, Stircaster.

Estate agent based in Stirton (Stoker and Galley Estate Agency).

Raised £30,325 for Cancer Research UK – late wife Gillian died from the disease aged 44 three years ago – chose the charity because of her.

Set off on February 18, ended on Saturday (November 24).

Started in Southampton on cold wet day, temperature close to freezing.

Finished in Southampton fresh but sunny day.

5,000 miles roughly.

Walked around 20 miles every day.

Met by his twin daughters Bryony and Tabitha (20) on sea front.

Bradley: "It was a very emotional moment when I spotted them in the distance as I came up to the finish point.

"I think all three of us were thinking about Gillian at that moment. It was very special."

"I had good days and bad days but when I felt tired and fed up I thought about my wife and the pain she went through towards the end of her life.

"I did this to help others in her position and hopefully the money I raised will do that."

Now thinking of walking the coast of France next year, starting and finishing in Monte Carlo. His wife wanted to go there but never did.

Slept in a camper van every night. Had relatives and friends driving to the next destination at the start of each day. They had a rota.

His brother James fell ill in June and couldn't get to north Wales to drive the van.

"I had to stay in a hotel when James didn't make it. The only place I could get a room was a five star hotel so that was a bit of a bonus."

Toughest stretch was the north-east coast of England – bleak views and still halfway to go at that stage so started flagging.

Best bit was west of Scotland and parts of Cornwall and Norfolk.

"Some of the views I had were absolutely wonderful. Many of the places I went through I had never been to before. I never realised what a beautiful country we live in."

Finished the walk two days early on what would have been Gillian's 47th birthday.

Had blisters in the early days of the walk but not after passing through Liverpool.

"I met some lovely people along the way. Some of them shared food with me, some bought me a beer and others just helped me pass the time by chatting as we walked."

Starts work again on Monday. His partner in the business has kept it going.

Exercise 3: Notes from a telephone interview with a teenager who was injured in a train crash which killed three people.

Research from BBC news website prior to interview:

The train which crashed was the 10.35am service from London King's Cross to Edinburgh Waverley.

Crashed into a stationary train as approached Newcastle station.

A woman aged 78, a man aged 35 and a female student aged 19 died.

37 people were injured. Three are still critical in hospital.

The accident is being investigated by Rail Accident Investigation Branch.

Tabloids have reported the driver had been seen drinking beer an hour before he started off on the journey.

Jessica Thompson (18), of Anderton Avenue, Stircaster.
Was travelling to Edinburgh to see friends.
Got on train at York. It collided with another train at Newcastle.

"There was quite a few people on the train.
"I've been on that route quite a few times.
"I go to see my friend Lizzie whose family moved up there."

"I feel lucky that I wasn't badly injured or worse. I could have been killed and I have to be thankful for that."

Jessica was going to cancel the trip the day before after falling ill.
Changed her mind when she felt better later.

Jessica: "I was reading my Kindle and had my headphones on listening to music.
"The train suddenly lurched and threw me forward against the table.
"I had a really bad pain in my ribs and my chest.
"Some people fell off their seats into the aisle.
"I don't remember much about what happened after that."

Broke three ribs, fractured wrist and bad bruising to her chest in the accident.

Parents (Phil and Wendy of Stircaster) rushed to hospital in Newcastle after she was taken there.

Been told she can come home tomorrow.

Just had A-level results – got A grades in English Literature, History and Politics at Stircaster Academy.

Had considered going to university in Newcastle to be near her friend.

Since decided to go to Warwick University.

Due to start at uni in three weeks. She hopes she will be well enough to go. Doesn't want to miss any of her course – BA in Political History.

Now compare your stories with how I have written them up. If you have used the structure I outlined earlier in this chapter you should have produced articles with great intros, solid supporting phases, a flowing main body and a satisfying conclusion to round them off.

Exercise 1 (sample story):

(intro)

A frustrated mum got so fed up waiting for the council to provide her with a disabled parking bay outside her daughter's school she spray-painted one on the road herself.

- This is such an unusual incident that you should lead off with it in your intro. Parents will sympathise with Mrs Grant not being able to park outside the school and many will admire her drive to do something about it.

(supporting phase)

> *Sophie Grant (32), of Stircaster, was unable to park near enough to Stircaster Primary School to be able to drop five-year-old Amy off safely on her first day of term on Tuesday because other parents had parked all the way along the street.*
>
> *She said she had been promised by Stirton County Council that a disabled space would be provided on Todderton Rise before the new term began.*
>
> *But it wasn't and because it made Amy late for her first day, Mrs Grant, of Letsby Avenue, decided to take matters into her own hands.*
>
> *"Amy chose a nice bright pink colour in B&Q and I went back to the school in the evening and sprayed a nice big parking space for myself," she said.*
>
> *"It felt really good to be doing something positive about the situation."*

- Here I have explained why Mrs Grant needs to park near the school and why she took such drastic action. Her quotes illustrate how she went about spray-painting the space and her emotions as she was doing it.

(body)

> *Mrs Grant, who is paralysed from the chest down following a car accident three years ago, drives an adapted car which allows her to use her wheelchair to get in and out.*

She said she decided to take action over the lack of a disabled parking bay when she was forced to drive around for 20 minutes looking for somewhere to park before eventually having to wait until other parents had driven away.

"It made me so angry because the council knew I needed that space," said Mrs Grant.

"I have to park near the school and then get my wheelchair out so I can safely take Amy to school.

"She's a little girl and I don't want to have to walk her miles to get to school every morning."

Tony Parmintor, head teacher of Stircaster Primary School, said he sympathised with Mrs Grant over the delay in providing the parking spot and said he would be pressing the council to put one in as soon as possible.

He said: "I can totally understand Mrs Grant's frustration over this. She clearly needs to be able to park near to the school to drop Amy off and collect her safely."

- Here I have gone into more detail about the frustrations Mrs Grant clearly felt and the fact she has highlighted an important issue for disabled parents. When there is a dispute of this kind you need to quote multiple sources because there might have been another side to the story. In this instance you need to give the school's version of events because it might otherwise reflect badly on them.

(concluding section)

The county council apologised for the situation and said it would be rectified this week.

A spokesman said: "We are very sorry about the trouble this matter has caused for Sophie and Amy.

"We were intending to paint on the disabled space in time for the start of the term but this wasn't done.

"The council would like to apologise for the inconvenience caused and we guarantee we will paint the parking bay in by the end of this week."

- The reader will now be asking about what is likely to happen and whether the parking bay will still be provided and they will also be interested to know why it wasn't provided in time. Had the council come back to us to say they had since painted in the parking space we would refer to that in probably the third sentence of the story but at the time of going to press or broadcast the official parking bay had still not been provided so this is added at the end.

Exercise 2 (sample story):

(intro)

A 51-year-old man from Stircaster has raised £30,000 for a cancer charity by walking around the entire coastline of the UK in memory of his wife who died from the disease.

- There are a lot of strands to this story all worthy of being included in the intro – the fact he has completed this amazing challenge, he's raised the colossal sum of £30,000 and all in memory of his late wife. The aim with any intro is to tell the story in as few words as you can, using dynamic words and phrases which grab the reader.

(supporting phase)

Bradley Stoker, a Stirton estate agent, arrived in Southampton on Saturday after completing his gruelling 5,000-mile challenge.

Memories of his late wife Gillian, who passed away three years ago at the age of 44, kept him going in his quest to raise money for Cancer Research UK.

He said: "I had good days and bad days but when I felt tired and fed up I thought about my wife and the pain she went through towards the end of her life.

"I did this to help others in her position and hopefully the money I raised will do that."

- The audience for this story will be wondering how he managed to pull this feat off and why he embarked on it. The lines here and the quotes explain it all nicely.

(body)

Bradley set off on his trek on a cold, wet day in Southampton on February 18. Friends and relatives worked on a rota to drive his camper van to the next destination each day so he could sleep in it when he arrived. He walked around 20 miles every day and, poignantly, he finished the walk two days early, on what would have been Gillian's 47th birthday.

When he walked the last few yards he was greeted by his 20-year-old twin daughters Bryony and Tabitha on the sea front.

"It was a very emotional moment when I spotted them in the distance as I came up to the finish point, said Bradley.

"I think all three of us were thinking about Gillian at that moment. It was very special."

He suffered from blisters in the early miles but had no problems with his fitness throughout the rest of the challenge.

The most difficult section, said Bradley, was the English north-east coastline because the views were bleak and because he still had half of the walk to complete.

He said he was indebted to the help and comradeship of those he met en route: "I met some lovely people along the way.

"Some of them shared food with me, some bought me a beer and others just helped me pass the time by chatting as we walked."

- You will notice I have called him Bradley rather than Mr Stoker and that is because there is a lighter tone to this story as opposed to one about a serious incident or issue. He has just finished the walk so we should aim to transport readers, listeners or viewers to that emotional moment on the sea front when he was greeted by his daughters at the finish. The human element to this piece should ensure your audience is engaged with the story from the start. We needed to explain some of Bradley's experiences on the trek and what he went through to complete the challenge during this phase of the story.

(concluding section)

Bradley is back at work at Stoker and Galley Estate Agency on Monday but he is already planning his next charity effort – a walk around the coastline of France, starting from Monte Carlo, where his wife dreamed of going but never went.

Meanwhile, he has some warm memories of his UK coastline challenge, particularly the stretches along the west coast of Scotland and parts of Cornwall and Norfolk.

Bradley added: "Some of the views I had were absolutely wonderful. Many of the places I went through I had never been to before. I never realised what a beautiful country we live in."

- The audience will want to know if he is going to do any other gruelling charity walks or whether this experience has put him off. It's also good to end with a quote reflecting on his experiences from a pretty unique achievement.

Exercise 3 (sample story):

(intro)

A Stircaster teenager has talked about the moment she was injured in a train crash which killed three people.

- We need to establish it was a young person from our patch who was injured and that the accident was serious enough to have killed some of her fellow passengers.

(supporting phase)

Jessica Thompson (18), of Anderton Avenue, was travelling to meet up with a friend when her train ploughed into the back of another stationary one at Newcastle station.

The former Stircaster Academy pupil broke three ribs, fractured her wrist and badly bruised her chest in the accident, in which a 78-year-old woman, a man aged 35 and a teenage girl all lost their lives.

"The train suddenly lurched and threw me forward against the table," said Jessica, who had been reading her Kindle and listening to music on her headphones.

"I had a really bad pain in my ribs and my chest. Some people fell off their seats into the aisle."

- This section explains why Jessica was on the train and what happened to her – this is a dramatic incident and you need to make the reader feel they are sitting close by her in the same carriage. The quotes from Jessica are strong enough to convey her shock at being involved in a serious incident.

(body)

Jessica, who said she remembered little about what happened next, was taken to Newcastle Infirmary to be treated for her injuries.

Her parents, Phil and Wendy, rushed to the north-east to be with their daughter.

Jessica, who got A grades this summer in her English literature, politics and history A-levels, is due to start a BA degree in political history at Warwick University in three weeks.

She has been told she should be able to go home tomorrow and is hopeful she will be well enough to start her course at the beginning of the new term.

- Here I have explained what happened to Jessica after her accident and the support she has had from her family. Look for the human angle in your stories.

(concluding section)

Jessica, who got on the train at York, was one of 37 people injured in the crash, with three remaining in a critical condition.

The Rail Accident Investigation Branch is investigating the incident, which involved the 10.35am from London's King's Cross to Edinburgh Waverley.

Jessica added: "I feel lucky that I wasn't badly injured or worse. I could have been killed and I have to be thankful for that."

- To round off the piece we need to refer back to the accident to add in any further details about it. Notice I have left out the reference in my research notes that the driver had been spotted drinking before driving the train. Unless this is substantiated in a court hearing it is legally dangerous to use even if some of the tabloids have highlighted it. Our story is about a local woman and how the accident has impacted on her life. These are great quotes from Jessica to conclude the article, showing her relief that her injuries were relatively minor compared to what other passengers sustained.

These templates give you a firm framework to build your stories on each time you start to write a new piece. Keep the different elements in mind when you go off on an interview. Ensure you have those killer quotes which you can use at the top of your story. And get the information you need to be able to round the article off effectively, so you can answer the questions your audience might have as a result of the subject matter you are writing about.

HEADLINE WRITING

Not that long ago newspaper and magazine reporters didn't have to concern themselves with writing a headline for their story.

That was done by a sub-editor, who designed the page, placed stories in the appropriate places according to their importance and wrote headlines in a bid to draw readers to each one.

Today, however, many titles have a publishing package where reporters write their story straight on to a page in specific story 'shapes'.

Not only do they have to make their copy sizzle but they also then have to supply a great headline to go with it.

This can be a bit daunting for some, especially those with little experience in the industry.

It can take a while to develop the knack of bashing out brilliant headlines every time.

Even the most experienced journalist may have to go back to a headline again and again to make the words fit and to convey the message they want to send out to their readership.

There are some hard and fast rules I have learned in my time as a sub-editor, sports editor and, latterly, a multi-media journalist, which I can share with you.

Follow these guidelines every time and you will soon develop a skill for making your headlines shine.

11 TOP TIPS FOR WRITING HEADLINES

1 Bring out the human element:

You should always be looking for the human angle because it will help readers engage more easily with the story.

So, include words like parents, teachers, traders, councillors, taxi drivers, police officers, firefighters and motorists, for example.

If the article is about an individual you might use their first name to personalise the piece but only use the surname in sports reports.

2 Use dynamic words:

Draw the reader's eyes in by throwing in some words which strongly illustrate the story.

If a train has crashed, for example, you might say it *smashed* or *ploughed* into a stationary train.

An organisation or an individual which has achieved something impressive will be *celebrating* and residents who have failed to prevent a big new development opposite their homes will be *angry* or *furious*. A street murder, for instance, may have resulted in the victim being *gunned down* rather than shot.

3 Include numbers or stats for effect:

It is a good idea when you have a story about a new school or hospital, for example, to include the cost in the headline. *'Pupils take first lessons in new £850,000 primary school'* will be more likely to catch the eye than *'New school open for first day of term'*. Put the cash prize in the heading when someone has won a Lottery jackpot or mention the percentage in the headline when you have a story about crime rates increasing drastically.

4 Include keywords for online searches:

Be aware when your story is also being uploaded to your publication's website because the headline is crucial in dictating how many people see it online. If a celebrity or a well-known film or television programme is mentioned in the story then make sure there is a reference in the headline. That will result in traffic coming in to your site from outside your patch because there is a wider interest and a higher searchability for your story. If the article refers to a town or village then get that in the heading, too, because readers will be searching for news from exactly where they live. In most cases you can write a separate headline for the printed publication and the website. It is important not to include the name of the same town or village too many times in headlines for the print version, though, or you will turn off readers who have no interest in that location.

5 Don't exaggerate for effect:

There is a great temptation to make more of something than is actually contained in the story.

You might have a story about a woman who bruised herself in a minor car accident. Now traffic smashes can, of course, kill people but if you were to write a headline such as *'Woman cheats death in car crash'* then it clearly does not reflect what happened in what was a low key shunt.

Similarly, a heading of *'Pensioner celebrates lottery windfall'* for a piece about a man who won a £10 prize with his weekly Royal British Legion draw would not accurately reflect what has happened.

6 Use active words:

When you use verbs in a headline make sure they are active. You want to convey a dynamic feel to your story to show it has recently happened or is happening now. For example, use *'Helen wins prestigious teaching award'* rather than *'Prestigious teaching award won by Helen'*. *'Police arrest a dozen drink drivers'* is also better to use than *'A dozen drink drivers arrested by police'.* For a story about striking cabbies you should write the headline *'Taxi drivers begin two-day strike'* as opposed to *'Two-day strike action begun by taxi drivers'.*

7 Stick to the facts:

It goes without saying that a headline must reflect the story it is promoting. Check the details in the story so you avoid putting something in the heading which is not in the story. This is particularly the case when you are paraphrasing a quote. If you have a story with few details about a road accident after which a motorcyclist was treated in hospital you might be tempted to write a headline along the lines of *'Motorcyclist rushed to hospital after serious road crash'.* The problem with this is that the biker may have been taken slowly to hospital if his injuries were severe to protect him from aggravating his injuries or it might have been a minor accident where he only suffered mild bruising. According to the scant facts you know, the headline should read 'Motorcyclist treated in hospital after road crash'.

8 Be sensitive:

I once wrote a tragic story about a girl who had committed suicide 10 days after her boyfriend was killed in a road accident.

The piece was a front page splash under the headline – written by a sub-editor colleague – *'Road death victim's sweetheart found dead in her bedroom'.*

A few hours after the paper was published the girl's father rang in to complain about the headline because he said it was too graphic and had upset the family.

I sympathised with him at the time but it was too late to change it, of course. A more sympathetic headline might be 'Family's grief over death of their teenage daughter'. Of course, graphic, insensitive headlines are commonplace in the tabloids but when you are starting your career on a local regional newspaper you need to be aware of the feelings of people living in the community you report on.

9 Look out for alternative meanings:

When you've written a headline, read it through again. And then read it one more time. It could be that something has gone into the heading which you didn't intend. A journalist friend tells the tale of one of his stories about a Dr Martin Fuchs, an eminent local archaeologist who had just secured his dream job in Italy. The sub-editor's headline was *'Dr Fuchs off to Rome'*. Now I'm guessing the sub did not intentionally write this as a joke but it clearly should never have made the published newspaper. Another headline I can remember being written, apparently in blissful ignorance, concerned a serious road accident where a motorist had an arm severed. The headline which appeared with the story was *'Man loses arm on hard shoulder'*. The connotations of linking the hard shoulder of the motorway with the man's horrific injury are terrible. It was a poor decision to use the words *hard shoulder* anyway as it is immaterial where it happened. *'Man loses arm in serious road crash'* would have more than sufficed in this case.

10 Don't replicate words from other nearby stories:

This is something many journalists overlook. There is nothing worse than picking up your latest newspaper or magazine issue and seeing two similar headlines for the lead stories on facing pages.

For example, you might have a story about exam results on the left-hand page with the headline *'Pupils celebrate record A-level results'* and then opposite on the right-hand page a piece about a local restaurant being awarded a Michelin Star under the heading *'Town restaurant's staff celebrate Michelin Star award'*. You don't want to use the same key word in facing headlines. It just looks a little unprofessional and it's not great from a page design viewpoint.

The same is true of using place names or a person's name in headlines on facing pages. If you have a village named in both stories or even a town the reader starts to think there is bias towards that location. And if you have two stories about *the Mayor* on opposite pages don't refer to the Mayor in both headlines. Ideally you would group the two Mayoral stories together on one page in any case. You want readers to think there is something interesting on every page and not a replication of stories with a similar subject matter.

11 Check your spellings:

Go through the story and check the spelling of names, places or organisations are the same in the headline as in the article. If you've not written the story yourself, check with the reporter. If you are unsure, then check the spelling online on an official website or by using a dictionary if it's a word. Check for typos too, of course, where you have unintentionally missed a letter or number out or added an extra one in. It goes without saying that if there are errors in the headlines of stories the professional reputation of your editorial team will quickly diminish with the readership. Mistakes like this also distract from great stories. The copy might be brilliant but if the headline has a glaring mistake in it then the impact of the story is often spoiled.

Good and bad headlines

To end this chapter we will compare good and bad headlines for the same story – if you've followed this section carefully you should be able to analyse why each one is either good or bad practice.

Good headlines:

- Villagers win battle to stop wind turbine plans

- Drink driver jailed after motorway pile-up

- Last orders for award-winning pub

- Brave gran Mary jumps out of a plane at 20,000 feet

- New £1 million hospital finally opens

- Jessica (9) rescues baby brother in swimming pool drama

- Councillor suspended after charity cash theft charges

- Traders blame new supermarket for falling business

- Firefighters rescue elderly couple from house blaze

- Rampaging bull injures farmers at weekly market

Bad headlines:

- Wind turbine plan blocked after villagers object

- Motorway crash driver sent to prison

- Village pub closes for business

- Parachute jump made by gran Mary

- Hospital open for patients after delay

- Baby saved by sister after falling into pool

- Councillor accused of stealing money is suspended

- 'Supermarket has lost us business' say traders

- Elderly couple escape fire thanks to fire service

- Farmers suffer injury after market animal escapes

These last two chapters will have given you a real understanding of what makes a great news story and a solid grounding on how you can become a top quality reporter for a news organisation.

Next I want to show you how to go about finding news. The development of the internet has made it a lot easier to source breaking news but the old traditional techniques of digging out stories still hold true, as we will see.

CHAPTER 4

HOW TO SOURCE NEWS – 19 TOP TIPS

CHAPTER 4: How to source news – 19 top tips

One of the main questions I am asked about my work as a journalist is simply: *How do you get news?*

People who don't work in the industry are fascinated about how a newspaper is filled up with stories, features and photographs reflecting life in the community it covers.

In my early years as a reporter there was no internet. In fact, there wasn't even a computer. I started out writing on a typewriter and the only way I could research articles was to telephone someone or consult a book in the office or the local library.

Trainee journalists today have a very different experience with the ability to look something up online in a matter of seconds.

There are also a multitude of communication channels to use. In a world before mobile phones and email it was often very difficult to contact key sources for stories if all you had was a home telephone number for someone or an address.

Today, of course, the majority of people have a mobile so they are easier to get hold of and many have access to their social media accounts throughout the day.

It's a totally changed landscape for the modern journalist which enables us to source more news easier and quicker.

This means, of course, that readers, listeners and viewers are eager to hear about breaking stories as soon as they happen or very shortly afterwards.

Reporters on weekly newspapers are now essentially working like journalists on dailies or 24-hour TV news channels.

And anyone who works in a print or broadcast outlet has a responsibility to provide a rolling news service, with a requirement to post the latest stories on their websites and on Twitter and Facebook feeds.

Exciting times indeed. And one of the reasons so many people want to get into the profession.

I felt it was important to devote a chapter of this book to the process of sourcing news stories and photographs. Here are 19 ways today's reporters unearth everything from mundane decisions taken at parish council meetings to world exclusives:

1 Press releases

News outlets are sent dozens of press releases every day.

Many of them are poorly written and little more than a request for a free plug for a new service or product.

Unfortunately, because news teams are often short of resources and they need to be publishing information throughout the day, more press releases are being used virtually word for word as they are written.

My tip would be to not take every press release on face value. There is often a better story buried somewhere in there, either because the press officer lacks the necessary news sense to bring it out or because they are trying to obscure something which might adversely affect their organisation's reputation.

The good news is that more journalists are making the crossover to public relations and as a consequence press releases are better written.

But it is as well to remember that they are still releasing essentially news with a bias towards their organisation. So in many cases you will need to get a comment or two from someone with an alternative view of an issue in the interests of balance.

2 Tweets

Every journalist should be on Twitter. This social media platform is a gift to reporters because it provides a rolling real time news service from relevant sources throughout the working day.

Newsrooms used to talk about a breaking item coming through on the wires from agencies such as Reuters or the Press Association.

Those companies are still running successfully but Twitter provides something very similar and it is totally free to use.

Local reporters should follow the accounts of every organisation, business and school in their patch and as many relevant prominent individuals as they can.

Keep an eye on your Twitter timeline and you will regularly see someone post something which is newsworthy and worth following up.

If you've cultivated a relationship with local users they will often tip you off by Tweeting a message to you or sending a private direct message which is not seen by the public.

By performing regular Twitter searches using keywords relevant to your patch you can get an insight into issues which are important to those who live and work there.

On one quiet news day I remember seeing a Tweet about smoke billowing around a town's high street. More posts followed on the same subject prompting us to send a reporter to the scene where a large garage was on fire.

Getting there early meant we could take dramatic photos and videos and speak to witnesses while the incident was still going on.

3 Emails

Like every workplace, it seems, journalists receive a large proportion of junk emails during the day.

But we do get more than our fair share of useful mails too. Stories can be turned around much quicker because you can be in email contact with a source rather than spending valuable time making telephone calls to them.

People who are pressed for time will often send a quick email to a newspaper or a broadcaster tipping them off about an interesting news item.

There will often be a contact daytime telephone number so you can follow it up when that person is available.

Readers will email in photographs of interesting events or incidents which are often better than those taken by your own staff or freelance photographer.

One of the most popular sections of local papers has always been the letters page, where readers make their own comments public on topical items.

Letters are often handwritten and many are littered with indecipherable words. But it is the case now that most letters are emailed in and consequently they are easier to read and process for publication.

Emails are also useful when you are short on news. Journalists will email their main contacts in the emergency services, at schools or at the council asking them for potential newsworthy material.

4 Facebook posts

Most news organisations now have their own Facebook page which contains a rolling timeline of stories.

The beauty of this social media platform is that readers can comment in detail and what they post can often change the angle of a story or prompt a follow-up.

It's important to keep an eye on your company Facebook site, though, because offensive language can occasionally be used, particularly in the aftermath of a controversial issue being reported. Such comments need to be moderated and removed immediately.

There are huge advantages to be had for newspapers and broadcasters from getting readers to 'like' their Facebook page.

Your aim should be to get them sharing content with their friends and encouraging people to get involved in topical debates.

They are potential sources of news. It's a bit like being able to eavesdrop on conversations between friends or colleagues in the pub or the coffee shop.

Occasionally something newsworthy will crop up and there will be times when a Facebook user will comment with something like 'the local paper should be reporting on this'.

Many organisations also use Facebook as their official website so by monitoring their messages you will pick up titbits which can be turned into news.

5 Letters

Despite the onset of the digital age there are some newspaper readers and radio listeners who send letters in for publication or broadcast.

Some of them will flag up potential news stories which deserve a higher profile than merely featuring on the letters page.

I can remember a reader's letter being sent to a former editor of mine where the author thanked a young woman for saving his life.

He had apparently suffered chest pains in the street and a passing teenage girl called an ambulance before comforting him in his distress.

The pair had kept in touch and we were able to follow up his letter with an interview and photograph with them both.

Councillors or high ranking police officers sometimes send letters in to highlight certain issues and they are also potential news stories if it is something that hasn't been covered before.

Passages from letters can also be used as part of news stories if readers are making relevant comments. In this case the full letter would still be published on the letters page in a newspaper.

6 Shop windows

I've often come across a story by seeing notices in shop windows while popping out for lunch or en route to another assignment.

As a journalist you need to be constantly aware of things around you which might be newsworthy.

A long established shop might put up a sign saying something along the lines of 'Unfortunately we are closing on Saturday after 36 years. Thank you to all of our regular customers'.

Clearly this is a good local story which can be followed up by interviewing the owner.

There might be a wider story to be had if they are in a particular trade which is losing out to the superstores or is no longer fashionable, for example.

Other notices might inform shoppers that the business is re-locating across town or that a new shop is opening up in a vacant unit.

People love to know what is going on in their city, town or village and so they lap up this kind of story.

7 Telephone calls

The volume of telephone calls to a news organisation has certainly gone down since the development of the internet but they still yield plenty of news stories.

Just when it appears to be a quiet news day you will get a call from someone telling you something which is worthy of the front page splash or the lead item on a bulletin.

The important thing to remember with calls is to make sure you get a contact number to be able to call them back to check something or ask additional questions.

This is particularly important if the line is poor and you suspect it might soon cut out. That has happened to me close to deadline and the caller did not call back for a story which was one of the best of the week.

Your older readers or listeners tend to want to use the telephone because they are not computer-savvy and it remains an important communication channel in this increasingly digital-orientated world.

8 Social events

You might be enjoying yourself at a dinner party or having a drink down the pub when something newsworthy happens or is spoken about.

A friend might have seen a serious road accident on his way to meeting you or another pal has heard that a major local employer is laying off staff.

You might see police arresting several people outside a nightclub or your cab driver could tell you about problems with motorists parking on the town's taxi rank and blocking it up.

These are all things you can make a mental note of or, perhaps, on your mobile phone to follow up when you are back in the office.

Editors love reporters who bring in stories so it will win you plenty of Brownie points and increase your chances of a future promotion.

You might be thinking at this stage that you might never get the chance to switch off and leave work behind you if you become a journalist.

But this isn't the case at all. It's just that you should get into the habit of thinking like a reporter and being aware of news when it happens around you.

9 Google alerts

This is a great little tool for getting updates on specific news issues whenever they appear online.

By setting up alerts around particular words, names or phrases you will get an email with a link to an article, website posting or blog as soon as it goes up on the web.

It's very simple to use. Go online at www.google.co.uk/alerts and you will arrive at a page with a search box containing the request to 'Create an alert about…'.

Then type in the name of a person you are interested in writing follow-up articles about. This might be a prominent personality in your patch, a criminal or a local celebrity, for instance.

You might also create a separate alert for an organisation, such as your local police force, district council or the largest employer in the area.

Another alert might be for a particular incident. So if you are covering a big fire at Heathrow Airport the phrase to type in might be 'Heathrow fire' and you will receive any online updates containing those words together.

Each time you create an alert you can also click the 'show options' tab which allows you to filter the search and confirm how often you want emails sent to you.

When you've entered the search words and selected the options another box will come up asking you to insert the email address you want alerts sent to.

Click 'create alert' and you will get regular updates which will help you keep on top of a story and move it on as it develops.

10 Follow-ups

Whenever you write a story which is likely to develop in future weeks you need to make diary notes to remind you at a later date.

These include, for example, court stories where there has been an adjournment or an appeal, articles on people preparing to do interesting charity challenges and planning applications set to be heard.

It's always worthwhile including a contact telephone or mobile number for a source on a story to remind yourself or so someone else in the office can pick it up.

Anniversaries of incidents or other stories covered previously also make good articles.

This is where the newspaper archive is particularly useful. Look back at the issue from exactly a year before and you will come across something to write about one year on.

It might be a child who is recovering from a serious illness, a person who survived being in the middle of a disaster or terrorist attack or perhaps a period of heavy flooding which damaged the homes of local people.

11 Contacts

Good contacts are worth their weight in gold in a newsroom. If you can build good relationships with key council officials or councillors they will tip you off about newsworthy stuff.

I have always tried to build trust with those working in the emergency services because they can give you the colour to your stories which will be missing if you rely on just the dry details released by a press officer.

If you are writing about a major fire you want to feature quotes from firefighters who were there to bring it to life.

The same goes for police officers. Detectives can let you know when people they have charged are due in court and they may also give you background to the case which you can use after it has gone ahead.

You must keep a contacts book and note down the telephone and mobile numbers of anyone you are likely to want to speak to again. Include a note about the organisation they represent or the issue you spoke to them about.

It's well worth keeping in touch with your main contacts even if it is the odd email to ask how they are or a message via social media. This will nurture a sense of trust in you which will bear fruit in the form of news somewhere down the line.

Beware of councillors and politicians telling you things because the news will often be heavily skewed towards the ethos of their party.

Such material can still be used but should be balanced with a view from an opposing political standpoint.

For example: You have been invited to attend the opening of a new academy which was formerly an established state school on your patch.

When you arrive you are greeted by the head teacher, as arranged, but the local MP is also there.

Now, the politician is a Conservative and the widespread creation of academies is an established Tory policy.

So by all means take down comments from the MP, which will inevitably be supportive about the new educational set-up.

But you should seek an alternative view, potentially from a parent who is disgruntled by the change, and also from a source with an alternative political perspective, to give the piece a sense of balance.

Remember, your job is to give readers both sides of an argument on the issues and topics you write about.

12 Notice boards

Town centres and village halls all have boards with updated information about local events and services.

They often reveal a fundraiser which you could write about or a celebration of a landmark to commemorate a milestone in its history.

The vicar might be holding his last service at the parish church or an appeal could have been launched to collect toys for orphans in a foreign country.

Of course you may come across these news items in the parish magazine or via a community website but you would be surprised how many newsworthy events are kept under wraps because someone has not had the time or the foresight to inform the local media.

13 Public meetings

Whenever you report on a public meeting called to oppose a controversial planning application, for example, or a recruitment drive for Neighbourhood Watch, the odd person will make contact with you.

Often this can be to relate a trivial occurrence which has no news value or someone will be keen to stir up trouble for an individual or an organisation they don't like.

Other people will feed you golden nuggets which can transform your night from reporting a dreary routine meeting to getting hold of information which can be followed up for a major story.

The tip-offs you get at public meetings are sometimes unconnected to the issues being discussed on the night.

And because members of the public don't regularly mingle with reporters they will make contact at meetings rather than taking the trouble to email the information or call a journalist on the telephone.

14 Anonymous tip-offs

Some stories require a lot more leg work when you first hear about them.

This is often the case when someone telephones the newsroom to tip you off that a councillor is being investigated for embezzling public funds, for instance, or that the air ambulance landed in someone's street to treat a neighbour.

Callers sometimes won't want to give their name or even their telephone number when it is sensitive information.

So you will then be forced to go to an official source to confirm the story.

The air ambulance incident is easy enough because the press office will have details of the call-out and the condition of the patient.

The embezzlement incident is much trickier since the council would be unlikely to give any details other than to confirm that a councillor has been suspended pending the outcome of an investigation.

There is still a good story there but you would be unable to go into any depth in the piece until the person is charged and appears in court.

15 Instagram photos

This particular social media platform is rising in popularity and now has more global users than Twitter.

By following the accounts of local organisations and prominent individuals you will get wind of newsworthy activities which may not have been relayed to the newsroom via another communication channel.

There are some excellent images posted regularly on Instagram and many are a good enough quality and high enough resolution to be used in a newspaper or on a broadcaster's website.

You should always ask whoever has posted a picture whether you can reproduce it in the paper or online.

Ideally, get them to email a bigger file size of the photograph and ask if you need to credit someone or an organisation.

At a time when fewer local newspapers retain staff photographers, Instagram images can be very useful particularly at a time when budgets are also being squeezed for freelance photography.

16 Websites

Many organisations release their news first via their website so it is as well to regularly log on to those of key institutions on your patch.

Police will post condition checks on victims of road accidents and the names of those who have been killed. They also make witness appeals for recent crimes or suspect descriptions.

Councils will give the results of planning applications which is particularly useful if no-one covered the latest meeting.

Schools are also now making good use of their websites to publish news items.

It is possible as well for reporters to glean newsworthy material off the sites of community organisations and action groups, among many others.

Much of this information will eventually make its way to the news desk via emails and press releases, but it will often appear first on an official website so they need to be monitored.

17 Other media

Don't ignore your rivals. They might be chasing the same stories as you and no matter how good a journalist you become they will still scoop you on occasions.

If you are working on a local weekly newspaper you need to see a copy of the rival daily covering your patch.

They will have stories in there which your publication has missed, simply because the source contacted them or they had better contacts.

Local radio stations often follow the news agenda set by the newspapers in their area but they do occasionally break big news, so it is worthwhile listening to their bulletins on a regular basis.

The same is true of local television news programmes. Their items tend to be targeted around the big cities in their region but there are often countywide issues which have implications for the area you report on.

The key with stories which have appeared elsewhere is to attempt to 'move them on' as we say in the industry.

That means finding a different angle or perhaps updating what a rival journalist has reported.

Sometimes there is nothing new to write about but there will still be value in publishing or broadcasting your story as many of your readers, listeners or viewers will not have been aware of the original piece.

18 Correspondents

Most local and regional newspapers have correspondents who collate and send in community news where they live.

This is a way for titles to cover some of the more rural areas without having to send reporters out there.

It's also good for the villages and hamlets to see their residents and organisations featuring in the local paper.

A lot of the copy features accounts of meetings of the women's institute, the parish council or the local gardening society.

There will also be minor fundraising items such as table top sales and pieces on fetes and family fun days.

This kind of news is referred to as the 'parish pump' and it is very popular with some sections of the readership.

It can also yield information which can be turned into page-leading news stories.

I can remember a village news item where the pensioner who supplied it had written about a shortage of bellringers in her parish.

Buried deep in the copy was the fact that five of the seven members had fallen pregnant.

This made a lovely story for the paper with a photograph of the expectant ladies holding the bell ropes in the church.

It was also interesting enough to win me our newspaper company's *Offbeat Story of the Year* award.

So you can see there are little gems hidden away in what otherwise looks like a mundane article.

19 Luck

Finally, we come to those fortunate occasions when you find yourself in the middle of a breaking story.

You might be in a long tailback caused by a serious car crash or an armed robbery might have taken place in the bank a few yards away from where you were buying a takeaway coffee.

These are extreme examples, of course, but it is a good idea to always carry a notebook, during the working day but also on your commute to and from work.

You never know when you might be on the spot to interview witnesses to a house fire or someone who has done something unusual such as parking his tank in a pub car park before going in for Sunday lunch.

That last one did actually happen, by the way, but it was the clever landlord, rather than a journalist, who took photos of the Army vehicle and its driver before sending them off to the media.

Then, of course, there are the rare occasions when a very famous celebrity appears on your patch unannounced.

In the late 1990s I was covering a tennis tournament in Buckinghamshire and was more than surprised to see the then Prime Minister Tony Blair turn up to present the trophies.

He had made the short journey from his weekend residence at Chequers but I made sure I got an interview with him after making the necessary enquiries and requests to his staff.

So be aware. The best stories can often land at your feet by pure chance.

This chapter gave you an insight into one of the biggest challenges facing all journalists – that of finding news.

Next we will look more closely at some of the specialist assignments you will be sent on as a reporter – covering court cases, inquest hearings and council meetings – and how you can do it effectively.

CHAPTER 5

COVERING COURT, INQUESTS AND COUNCIL MEETINGS

CHAPTER 5: Covering court and council meetings

One of the biggest early tests of a young journalist's mettle comes when they are asked to cover a court hearing for the first time on their own.

When I started out I was able to shadow an experienced reporter covering cases at magistrates' and crown courts and this is still the case with many news outlets.

But, as newsroom resources shrink, more and more rookies are being sent to report the courts with just a short informative pep talk by the editor behind them.

It can be extremely daunting going into these places with little or no previous experience.

And it can take several stints and many weeks before a young reporter feels confident in this often highly charged environment where crucial life-changing decisions are taken in the lives of those affected by the cases.

There is a certain protocol and I thought it would be useful to give a few pointers to make the experience much less painful for those thrust into the challenge of court reporting.

FIVE TOP TIPS FOR COVERING COURT CASES

1 Read up on newspaper law

This might sound obvious but it is crucial that you keep up with legislation which defines what you can and can't report.

The best thing you can do is invest in the latest edition of *McNae's Essential Law for Journalists*. This is the law Bible for reporters and contains everything you need to know.

Keep an eye on changes to the laws as well via industry titles such as the UK Press Gazette or the website www.holdthefrontpage.co.uk .

Cases are initially heard in magistrates' courts, which have the power to hand out a maximum six-month prison sentence and fines of up to £5,000.

There will often be several preliminary hearings, to give legal teams more time to prepare their case or for reports to be made on the state of mind of a defendant, for example.

Background information about the case will often be given out but until the hearing is properly heard and a verdict delivered by magistrates there are only certain details you can report at this stage.

This is merely the name of the defendant, their age and address, the offence they are charged with and where it took place, plus the date of the next hearing and bail arrangements.

These limitations are in place to prevent any future jury trial being prejudiced by early publication of the particulars of the case.

There are occasions, however, when these reporting restrictions might be lifted by magistrates to allow more of the case to be reported.

Magistrates deal with nine out of 10 cases but more serious offences, such as murder, rape and robbery, are dealt with by judges in crown courts.

The same reporting restrictions apply to these hearings until the case is heard and a verdict delivered by a judge or jury.

If you are asked to cover youth courts, you cannot report the names of the juvenile defendants who are aged under 18 or any material likely to lead to their identification.

2 Increase your shorthand speed

If you've been taken on as a trainee you might be given training in shorthand to allow you to take notes more quickly when interviewing people or covering meetings and hearings.

Shorthand will also be taught as part of a journalism degree or a National Council for the Training of Journalists (NCTJ)-approved training course.

But if you are trying to get into journalism without any previous experience or training I would strongly advise you to enrol on a course at your local college.

Most journalists use Teeline outlines which allow you to take notes at speeds of up to 150 words a minute.

Being proficient at shorthand is absolutely essential for court reporting. It is illegal to make an audio recording of the proceedings.

You need to be able to take clear and precise notes of what is said because if you get it wrong the penalties can be severe both for yourself and for the news organisation you represent.

Building high speeds with shorthand gives reporters the confidence they can quote defendants, witnesses and legal professionals to give that all important colour to their court copy.

People speak at different speeds and generally they quicken up when they are nervous or under pressure, as they are in court hearings, so you need to have the note-taking skills to respond to this.

Even the quickest shorthand writers don't always get an accurate note, however, because they didn't hear clearly or their pen ran out of ink, for example.

So don't be afraid, as a young journalist or a trainee, to ask a more experienced reporter on the press benches for assistance if you miss an important passage of the hearing or you are worried you didn't take it down correctly.

Most will be happy to help, provided you don't consult them every five minutes!

Trainee journalists will often be the only member of the press in court. You can check details of the case with the prosecuting counsel or the clerk during a lull in proceedings but, if you are unsure about a quote you have made a note of, it is advisable not to use it.

Court reporting is covered by a legal term called qualified privilege, which means you can safely report anything which is said in the hearing (where a verdict is reached) by defendants, witnesses or legal professionals.

So you can use a quote where a woman alleges a man assaulted her, for instance, or when someone accuses another person of stealing from them.

The qualified privilege legal defence is valid if your report is fair, accurate, created without malice, subject to a right of reply and contemporaneous (published in the next available printed issue or public broadcast).

Covering court stories can be challenging if the subject matter is bleak and depressing. But it can also be incredibly exciting when you are hearing the events of a major case played out in front of you before getting the opportunity to tell the world about it.

I would advise anyone seriously thinking of a career in journalism to start their shorthand training as soon as possible, particularly if they want to specialise in covering the courts for national newspapers, radio stations or television news channels.

3 Get there early and access the court register

It takes time to get through security checks at courthouses these days.

When I started out you just wandered through the front door and made your way into the courtroom but these days the entrance is more like an airport customs area where you are checked for weapons or anything likely to disrupt proceedings. So reporters need to be there early.

When you've made it through security, head for the court office to get your copy of the register, the schedule of cases for the day.

This will tell you where particular defendants are due to appear, if there are multiple courtrooms, and whether it will be during the morning or afternoon session.

The document will also give you the defendant's date of birth, current address, any plea they have made, brief details about the charge they face and the stage the hearing has reached.

This, of course, is all vital information for your story.

In court reporting the full address is given in stories unlike in most other news reports. This is to avoid readers associating the case with someone else who has the same name and who lives in the same city, town or village.

If you have arrived late in court, for whatever reason, you can usually get hold of a spare copy of the schedule from a court usher.

And if you arrive as a court case is being heard, do so quietly and respectfully.

4 Build a relationship with court staff

Your main port of call as a journalist is the court usher, who you will see regularly entering and leaving the courtroom clad in black robes.

Introduce yourself to them and tell them who you are and which news organisation you work for.

They are usually keen to help, supplying spare court registers or giving you information about particular defendants and what approximate time they are likely to appear during the day.

Ushers are also useful for giving the names of solicitors, barristers, magistrates and judges if you want to quote them but are unsure what their names are.

Prosecutors and defence counsel are also generally approachable but if you want to check anything with them make sure it is during a recess between cases.

Court cases always follow the same protocol so it is a good idea to familiarise yourself with the order of things:

- The defendant will be called first and then the court clerk, who sits just in front of the magistrates or judge, will read out their name and the particulars of the charges against them.

- The defendant will be asked to make a plea although in preliminary hearings they do not have to at that stage.

- The prosecution, representing the Crown Prosecution Service (CPS), will then outline the case giving details of what happened and how the offence occurred.

They will also call for certain penalties to be delivered in the event of a guilty verdict, such as imprisonment or a large fine.

- The defence solicitor, or barrister in a crown court hearing, will then argue the case for the defendant and offer any mitigating evidence.

It's important you make reference to this information in your report, even if the defendant has pleaded guilty or is found guilty after a trial.

- There may be some cross-examination from both sides before the magistrates, or the judge, retire for a period of time to consider their verdict or the sentence if a guilty plea has been entered.

- When a verdict is delivered, listen carefully and make a clear note of it. Check it later with the court clerk or prosecutor if you are unsure about what was said.

Sometimes you might want to talk to a defendant after the hearing, if it is a high profile individual, or to victims or witnesses who have been affected by the case.

Approach them outside the courtroom, preferably, but be prepared for a refusal and, on occasions, a rebuke in response to your enquiry.

You are forbidden from taking either photographs or video footage of any activity inside the court room or inside the court house.

Defendants, witnesses and legal professionals can be photographed or filmed outside the building.

Members of the jury, if you are covering a trial, should never be identified in your reporting of a case.

5 Make connections with rival court reporters

Young journalists are often surprised about how friendly reporters from rival news organisations are with each other.

But you are doing the same job and often journalists might have worked together at one stage.

That doesn't mean you don't try to write a better story than your rival and you don't give important information away which might spoil your exclusive story.

But reporters will often compare notes in court, such as the exact wording of a quote, the length of a sentence handed down from 'the bench' or the address of a defendant.

So don't be afraid to make friends with the regular court reporter from another newspaper or broadcaster.

They will come in handy at some stage and in certain circumstances might be the difference between you getting an important story or failing to get it.

Experienced journalists are often keen to pass on their knowledge and expertise so if you are unsure about something go ahead and ask them, no matter how inexperienced and naive it may make you look.

So, just to recap, here are the main things you should be doing when you cover the courts and also some things you shouldn't do:

Do –
- Get there early to avoid delays with security checks
- Collect a court schedule from the admin office
- Check with the usher when specific defendants are appearing
- Make contact with legal professionals only during a break in proceedings
- Check case details with rival reporters
- Only approach defendants/witnesses for comments outside the courtroom

Don't –
- Cause a distraction if you arrive while a case is in progress
- Attempt to speak to the magistrates or the judge at any time
- Speak to legal professionals while a case is in progress

- Include details of the case which you are not sure about
- Spell the name of a defendant wrongly or put the wrong address in
- Take photographs or video footage in court or in the foyer

THE ROLE OF A REPORTER AT INQUESTS

An inquest is held by a coroner – sometimes assisted by a jury – to investigate the causes of an unexplained, sudden or violent death.

It can also look into discoveries of historical artefacts or valuable materials to establish the legal owner and whether that person is still alive to claim it.

But journalists are mainly concerned with inquests relating to deaths.

And the important thing to remember is that the coroner is not appointed to assign blame but merely to establish the facts and the contributing factors.

Inquests are generally held in courthouses and resemble court cases in many aspects.

The coroner takes witness statements from people who speak after taking the oath.

Solicitors for the family of the deceased can cross-examine witnesses on the evidence they have given.

At the end of the hearing, the coroner will give his verdict, which might be 'accidental death', 'death by natural causes', 'death from an industrial disease' or an 'unlawful killing'.

Occasionally, there will be an 'open verdict' which means that doubt remains over how that person died.

The coroner might also find that 'he killed himself while the balance of his mind was disturbed'.

Clearly, these hearings can often be incredibly emotive for family members and witnesses who saw someone lose their life.

It goes without saying that journalists are required to respect the proceedings and the people involved in them.

That means not pestering those who are visibly distressed by what has happened when you are looking for a reaction to the verdict. You can always contact members of the family later on when they have had a chance to digest the hearing.

On occasions, people will be keen to speak to the media directly after an inquest and in some cases a press conference might be held outside the courthouse or wherever the hearing has taken place.

The coroner's officer will be on hand, as ushers are at court hearings, to confirm the spelling of names and the addresses of those who speak at an inquest.

And a press bench will be made available for members of the media.

HOW TO COVER COUNCIL MEETINGS

They may not be high up on your list of reasons for going into journalism but council meetings have to be covered and they often yield very important community stories.

Trainee journalists will cut their teeth reporting on county, district or borough council committees and they may also be assigned parish council meetings in busy news areas of the patch.

Media organisations are sent agendas for the various meetings, usually via email these days in a bid to cut costs and appear more environmentally friendly.

Once a month, district councils hold a full council meeting where councillors will consider recommendations made at the authority's various committees.

The best stories often come out of planning meetings, particularly when a contentious scheme is discussed such as a giant wind turbine or a large development of houses.

These are also the only meetings which are well attended by the public, usually because action groups are often set up to oppose certain plans.

They are good community stories where you will find affected residents are eager to pass comment to newspaper and broadcast reporters.

You will see the same faces protesting in certain areas - these are the so-called NIMBY (Not In My Back Yard) residents you can rely on for a quote when a controversial planning application is lodged.

Other committees discuss environmental issues, community and social affairs, policy and finance, licensing matters and housing.

There is a similar structure to county council meetings, although their committees relate to their spheres of influence, such as highways and transportation, education and social services.

Parish councils tend to meet once a month although their powers are largely restricted to making recommendations on issues to district and county councillors.

In terms of covering council meetings, you need to be aware of when agendas are sent out for the various meetings.

These can be used as the basis of stories ahead of the meeting when, for example, an officer has made a recommendation on a subject which is set to be discussed.

Let's assume you have been sent out on an assignment to cover the district council planning meeting for the very first time. This is what you need to do:

- Read the agenda thoroughly and make a note of planning applications which are likely to be newsworthy.

- Print out the details on those plans so you can refer to them at the meeting.

- If you've not been to a council meeting before, go online to their website and familiarise yourself with what individual members of the planning committee look like so you can quote them in your articles.

- Get to the meeting 10 minutes early and introduce yourself to members of the committee and to members of the public, some of whom may want to comment after the meeting.

- Sit at the press table – there will be one set aside for the media close to where the councillors sit and slightly away from the public gallery.

- Follow the discussion on each of the planning applications which interest you and try to take quotes down from members who have contrasting opinions.

- Make a note of how many councillors vote in favour of a planning application and those who oppose it – it can often be a decision taken by a single majority vote, which will add an extra angle to your story.

- There will often be a break in proceedings for refreshments so use this to speak to councillors if you need to confirm or query anything or to make contact with members of the public who want to comment on a controversial scheme. This can also be done at the end of the meeting.

- Write separate articles on each of the interesting items on the agenda – these reports attract a lot of hits on the website because they are often important community issues residents care passionately about.

The content in this chapter will have given you the confidence to go into courthouses and council chambers and produce great reports even if you have never set foot in either before.

In the next chapter I will give you some pointers on how to write fantastic features.

CHAPTER 6

HOW TO WRITE
GREAT FEATURES

CHAPTER 6: How to write great features

Writing news stories is very formulaic in that there is a rigid structure you should adhere to when putting together your articles.

Features are slightly different because they are often lighter in subject matter, longer in word length and they give the reporter an opportunity to inject some of their own personality and writing style into them. I've always enjoyed writing features for this very reason.

You will invariably have the chance to meet the subject of your feature face-to-face and spend time talking to them.

This contrasts dramatically with news stories which are often constructed after two or three phone chats with sources and then written up swiftly, particularly when you are approaching deadline.

Some journalists find feature-writing difficult and it is true that some are better at it than others.

There is a knack to doing it well, however, and later in this chapter I will set you two exercises where you will get a chance to write features based on sets of made-up notes from an interview.

You should pick up plenty of tips to help you churn out entertaining and interesting features.

Some of the guidelines I outlined in Chapter 3, when we looked at the building blocks of a story, are relevant but there is a looser format to feature writing which makes it a unique skill in its own right.

Firstly, I will run through the key components you will find in every good feature.

The 8 essential ingredients of a good feature article

1 A great image

This is where the skill of a professional press photographer comes in – capturing an image which is interesting enough to draw the reader into a feature.

Because this kind of article is usually considerably longer than a news story it requires a bigger investment of time for anyone who is reading your publication.

The feature might also be on a subject which is of no interest to a particular reader but if it is accompanied by a particularly striking image they may well be drawn in.

The driest of topics can become fascinating if they are illustrated dynamically. I recall writing a feature about a fundraising campaign to replace the bells in a historic church. Our photographer made the precarious journey up a steel ladder to get into the bell tower and she produced a stunning shot of the church warden crouching beneath one of the giant old bells.

By the same token, I can recall feature photographs which have been duller even than the subject they were attempting to depict.

If you take the picture yourself have a look at Chapter 8 for some tips on how to take press photographs but also try to think outside the box. Look for quirky shots like the reflections of people in a classic car's wing mirror or shooting from an unusual angle, up from ground level or high up and looking down.

Of course, if the writing isn't very good then even the best photograph ever taken is unlikely to retain the attention of readers but if you can get both elements right then it will add real value to that issue of your newspaper or magazine.

2 An intriguing headline

A good headline is important for any article in a printed publication or on a news website because it is the gateway to the story about to be read.

As with the writing style for features, compared to news stories, you can be more creative and inventive with your headline.

A good photograph will draw the eye in and if the headline is equally as beguiling that should be enough to entice the reader to consider reading the feature.

Ideally, focus in on a human interest angle or something off-beat and unusual. Humorous headlines work well on features as does a good 'play on words' providing it's not too clichéd or cheesy.

For serious news features – such as an extended look at an issue which was the subject of a front page report the previous week – it is advisable to write a headline more in keeping with the subject matter, while still making it interesting enough to gain the reader's attention.

Here are a few examples of headlines which work well with specific features:

IT'S CHOCKS AWAY FOR HAROLD AS HE TAKES TO THE SKY ONCE MORE

(Feature about a former Second World War Spitfire pilot who is taken for a spin in a light aircraft 50 years after his last flight)

VETERAN BEACH LIFEGUARD JIMMY DRAWS A LINE IN THE SAND

(Feature about a pensioner who has retired from duties after a lifetime looking after swimmers on a Norfolk beach)

SCHOOLGIRL SARAH LOVES HER 'JAM AND JERUSALEM'

(Feature about a 14-year-old who is the youngest member of a village Women's Institute group by 36 years)

PART-TIME PARAMEDICS WHO LEAD A DOUBLE LIFE TO HELP SAVE LIVES

(Feature about Community First Responders who are trained to assist the emergency services while holding down a job in another profession)

3 A standfirst

This is the short one or two-paragraph passage editors sometimes insert at the start of a feature.

It's another trick to draw the reader in and also serves to show this article is something different from news stories in a publication.

It's usually written in a different font from the feature and is bolded up to make it stand out.

The standfirst gives the reader a short precis of what the piece is about, as well as mentioning anything relevant which has appeared in recent issues. The writer's by-line will also be included in the text.

The following might be used as standfirsts for features:

70 years ago Londoners celebrated VE Day and the end of the Second World War in Europe.

Stanley Webb didn't join in the celebrations, however, because he had lost too many friends and comrades in the fighting. *SALLY HARRISON* talks to Stanley about his war and why he can't forget those who didn't make it through alive.

Harriet Smith spends her life looking after animals and her job is a real labour of love. She has worked as a vet in Nottingham for 25 years and at home she cares for three donkeys, two horses, three dogs, two cats and a rabbit. *MATT HOWARD* finds out where her love of animals comes from.

4 A captivating intro

So, you've got a brilliant photograph, a fascinating headline and a punchy standfirst. But don't let up because you've now got to kick your feature off with an intro which really grabs the attention of your reader.

It is often well worth posing a question and making your audience think about the issue or topic you have written about.

Something like:

How many pints would you guess were served at Leicester's annual beer festival over the Bank Holiday weekend?

You would probably be surprised to learn it was a remarkable 12,000.

You might also consider what is called a 'drop intro' – a paragraph which states something newsworthy without it being qualified or backed up by anything. The second par would then attribute the claim to an individual or organisation. An example of this is:

The build-up of dog poo in Manchester parks is causing a serious health risk to children who play there.

That was the claim made by the city council's director of parklands, Bill Maguire, who has just completed 25 years' service in the role.

Another option for an intro is to put the reader in the shoes of the subject.

This might take the form of:

If you were faced with a drunken angry individual what would you do?

Well, Stephen Franklin has to deal with that challenge just about every Saturday night as a police officer patrolling Oxdown city centre.

(an intro for a feature with a police officer who patrols inner city streets on busy nights)

5 Dynamic early quotes

If you've managed to come up with a great intro to your feature then the first quotes you use will back up that opening statement.

There's an old adage which says that newspaper readers only read the opening three or four paragraphs of most stories.

If they aren't hooked by then they will look elsewhere on the page for another article or turn to the next page.

This is particularly true when it comes to features because the reader is faced with a 400 or 500-word piece to get through compared to the 250 or 300 words usually devoted to page lead news articles.

So you need to be on the lookout for good quotes from the moment you start interviewing someone for your feature.

Here are some examples of great quotes to back up the introduction on totally fictitious features.

Feature 1:

Most people form their opinion of the Queen on what they see from television or media coverage, but St Albans pensioner Henry Thompson considers her a friend.

The 81-year-old trained her racehorses for more than 40 years and he has spent many hours with her during that time.

He talks with pride at the laughs they shared and the occasional disagreements as he looks back on his memorable career.

"The Queen has a wicked sense of humour," said Henry, who has three children and eight grandchildren.

"She had me in fits of laughter on occasions and I almost forgot at times that I was having a laugh and a joke with the Queen of England."

Feature 2:

Some actors go through their whole career without getting a major role but Helen Chambers landed her dream part at her first ever audition.

The 18-year-old, from Barnsley, will play a villain in the latest James Bond movie, which is due out this summer.

She took part in dramatic car chases and tense scenes with the star of the show himself, Daniel Craig.

> Helen said: "I was very nervous on set on the first day but Daniel and all the other actors made me feel relaxed.
>
> "It is literally a dream come true. I have seen all the movies and I can't believe I'm actually going to be in one myself."

Feature 3:

Sometimes your quotes are so good they are worthy of acting as the introduction to your feature.

This can be a powerful way to draw the reader in from the very start.

Like this:

> "When you are out in the ocean, totally alone, it is the best feeling in the world but it is also scary because all you can see for miles and miles is the sea around you."

That was how Brian Saunders described his remarkable feat of sailing twice around the world continuously.

The 34-year-old gave up his career as an estate agent to follow his passion for sailing and he has now travelled more than 100,000 nautical miles across the globe in the last five years.

6 A flowing writing style

The body of the feature really needs to flow. This is an element of journalism when you can inject your own personal writing style into articles.

The tone of your piece will be determined by the subject matter. So if you are writing about a serious issue then a more formal, authoritative vibe should come through in your writing.

If the feature is about someone who has achieved something noteworthy or they have a unique skill or talent then a lighter, more conversational tone can be adopted.

Occasionally you will write offbeat features about unusual or quirky characters and in this case your writing can have an emphasis which is more humorous or wry.

You can be inventive as well. Try putting in very short sentences now and then to set up an important point you are about to make or to break up the words to make life more interesting for your readers.

Ask questions in your piece, as you would have done during the interview. And then give the answer in the next par.

Have a look at your local newspaper or lifestyle magazine and see how they structure their feature articles.

A great way of developing your own distinctive feature writing style is to start your own blog.

You can set up a free one on sites such as *WordPress, Tumblr* or *Blogger* and then try to post a fresh blog every two weeks. Write about something you are passionate about or a topical news issue and if you keep at it you will be amazed how quickly your writing confidence will increase.

7 Fact or stat boxes

This is another useful element editors sometimes use to break up the words of a lengthy feature and to help attract readers to it.

It's particularly effective when your article includes a barrage of facts and figures or statistics.

By putting some of the figures in separate boxes around the piece it can help to emphasise some of the interesting points you are trying to get across.

I wouldn't advocate using them on every feature you write but they are worth considering for certain pieces.

The following are all content which could be considered for fact or stat boxes in features:

Feature on a road accident black spot:

Accident figures for Cedar Hill junction since 2010

Number of fatal accidents – 5

Number of serious injury accidents – 12

Number of minor injury accidents - 24

Feature on a revitalised seaside resort:

Summer holiday visitors (hotel bookings) 2005 – 46,464

Summer holiday visitors (hotel bookings) 2015 – 74,566

Percentage increase in 10 years – 64%

Feature on closure of popular cinema:

Opening date: March 4, 1973

First film shown: Last Tango in Paris

Longest run for a film: Star Wars (3 weeks, 1977)

Last film shown: Mission: Impossible – Rogue Nation (August 5, 2015)

8 A concluding summary of what the feature has revealed

There is a real skill to rounding off a feature – to end with a line which sums up everything the reader has just taken in.

Sometimes your summary will take the form of an appropriate quote or occasionally it will be just your own words.

The best way of doing it is to revisit your intro and the opening lines.

Did you pose a question at the start? If so, you need to answer it in the final par, drawing together information which the feature has provided.

Did you introduce an individual and their skill or claim to fame? If this is the case then you should refer back to it and emphasise the significance of what they have achieved.

The aim is to finish your feature in a satisfying way and validate why it was worthwhile writing it.

Here are some great ways of signing off at the end of a feature.

Feature on policeman who has served 30 years in the same rural town:

And does Mr Smith have any regrets that he never served in another more challenging area of the country?

"Not really," he added. "I grew up here. People here are my friends and I would like to think I have made a big difference to their lives by helping to keep their homes and their businesses safe from crime."

Feature on man who collected more than 100 classic cars:

Mr Jones admitted his hobby had got out of hand at times with not enough space at his family home to park them all.

But he doesn't regret buying any of the vehicles, particularly his favourite one.

"I paid £22,000 for my 1967 Jaguar," he added. "If I had to give them all back bar one I would keep the Jag because it looks so incredibly amazing."

Feature on nation's biggest Olly Murs tribute act:

When asked why so many fans come to see him rather than the real Olly Murs, Johnny is in no doubt about the answer.

He said: "People who like Olly can come to my gigs for a fraction of the cost and they will still hear all their favourite tunes and have a great time. I will keep singing as Olly for as long as the fans want me to."

Feature writing exercises

It is now time to put into action the pointers I have given about how to write quality features with a challenge to you to write two of your own.

With both of these assignments, look through the notes and then write your own feature articles, based on the key components previously outlined in this chapter.

Then take a look at the specimen features I have written based on both of these sets of notes – you can compare your efforts with mine to help get an understanding of what goes into this kind of writing.

Make sure you do some online research to get your facts right about the subject matter if you need to.

1st Feature brief:

To interview former Second World War Spitfire pilot Sydney Lawrence to mark the 75th anniversary of the Battle of Britain

Date and time:

September 9, 2015 at 3pm

Notes taken:

Sydney Lawrence (96), of Trumpington Close, Cambridge.
Late wife was called Constance (died 8 years ago).
Two children – Terrence (69) & Marilyn (67).
Six grandchildren.
Seven great-grandchildren.

Sydney joined RAF in 1938 and trained as a pilot.
Based at RAF Biggin Hill during the Second World War.
Stayed in the air force throughout the war but left at the end of it.

"I always wanted to fly. It fascinated me as a child how these planes could stay in the air.
"When I joined the RAF I knew there was a chance I would have to fly in combat but I just wanted to fly."

Sydney is a member of the Royal British Legion in Cambridge. Tries to get down to the club once a week.

Used to have reunion dinners with colleagues from his wartime squadron until late 1990s but he is the only one still alive of those he stayed in contact with.

"I've seen Spitfires flying at air shows and it does bring back memories. I can remember scrambling to get in mine whenever there was an air raid siren going off. It was exciting. I wasn't nervous. I was a young man so it didn't frighten me.

"When we started losing planes it did make you start to think. I lost a lot of good friends. But we had a job to do. If we didn't stand up to the Luftwaffe that would have been it for our country."

Sydney's first flight in a Spitfire was in 1939 shortly after war broke out. He didn't engage any enemy planes.

First time he faced up to an enemy aircraft was over the English Channel in May 1940 – he shot down a Messerschmitt Bf 109 during a dogfight.

"The heart was pumping and the adrenaline was going like the clappers.

"It was him or me and luckily it was him.

"I didn't sleep that night. Not because I shot that plane down but the adrenaline was still pumping and I was still on a high.

"It was hard to sleep in the summer that year. We had to be ready for the Luftwaffe and we knew how important our role was."

Sydney met Constance at a tea dance in Bromley while on leave in winter 1942.

She was very emotional every time he went back to his base. She knew the dangers.

Constance worked in a school in London and survived The Blitz while living in Dagenham.

"Connie was hardened to the war. She was right in the middle of it when the Germans bombed London. The whole of her street was flattened and she lost many friends."

Sydney worked as a gas fitter after the war.

He married Constance in 1945, a week after VE Day.

Their first child was born a year later (Terrence).

"We lived in a little terraced house in Croydon. Life was hard but we were happy. We were thankful we won the war. I didn't feel like a hero though. No-one treated me any different in the street. Everyone played their part, like Churchill said."

Sydney also worked as a milkman and a postman in later years.

He retired in 1989 but still worked part-time as a lollipop man outside Trumpington Primary School.

He enjoyed the film The Battle of Britain but thought a lot of it wasn't realistic.

Doesn't like watching war films now.

"War films glamorise war and there is nothing glamorous about war."

Has attended remembrance parade in Cambridge every year. Will continue to do while he is fit enough to do it.

- Now have a go at writing your feature based on these notes before taking a look at the specimen feature I have written. Compare your efforts with my article. Like many things, practice makes perfect but if you follow my guidelines you will soon be confidently bashing out top quality features on a regular basis.

1st Specimen feature:

(headline):

CAMBRIDGE PENSIONER REMEMBERS HIS BRAVE ROLE IN THE BATTLE OF BRITAIN

(standfirst):

75 years ago Hitler tried to destroy the RAF in an attempt to make way for the German invasion of these islands. Our pilots were heavily outnumbered but they heroically defied the enemy in what became

known as the Battle of Britain. Sydney Lawrence was one of them and he told NICK RENNIE about his incredible experiences.

(introduction):

It was one of the momentous events in our nation's history – how the RAF courageously defeated Hitler's all-conquering Luftwaffe in the Battle of Britain.

But what was it like to be in a Spitfire, right in the thick of the action as our pilots duelled with the enemy over southern England and the English Channel?

Cambridge pensioner Sydney Lawrence knows exactly what it was like and 75 years on he can remember the experience like it was yesterday.

(dynamic opening quotes):

"It was exciting," the 96-year-old recalled. "I wasn't nervous. I was a young man so it didn't frighten me.

"When we started losing planes it did make you start to think. I lost a lot of good friends. But we had a job to do. If we didn't stand up to the Luftwaffe that would have been it for our country."

(flowing body of the feature):

Sydney, who lives in Trumpington Close, had only joined the RAF two years previously. He knew war was approaching and that he would be risking his life when he signed up for flight training.

"I always wanted to fly," he said. "It fascinated me as a child how these planes could stay in the air.

"When I joined the RAF I knew there was a chance I would have to fly in combat but I just wanted to fly."

Britain declared war on Germany in September 1939 and eight months later Sydney engaged an enemy aircraft for the first time – a Messerschmitt Bf 109 over the English Channel. Henry's eyes watered as he remembered the dogfight and the moment he shot down the Luftwaffe plane.

"The heart was pumping and the adrenaline was going like the clappers," he recalled.

"It was him or me and luckily it was him. I didn't sleep that night. Not because I shot that plane down but the adrenaline was still pumping and I was still on a high."

Sydney was based at RAF Biggin Hill during the Second World War. Life was tense knowing that every day could be his last.

Going out on leave was the only release he and his fellow pilots had and on one trip outside the base he met a girl called Constance at a tea dance at Bromley.

The couple began dating but she was very emotional every time they parted. She knew the dangers he faced every time he climbed into his cockpit.

Constance worked as a teacher in a school in London and survived the devastating bombing of the Blitz while living in Dagenham.

"Connie was hardened to the war," Sydney recalled. "She was right in the middle of it when the Germans bombed London. The whole of her street was flattened and she lost many friends."

Thankfully, the couple both survived the war and they married in 1945, a week after VE Day.

Their first child, Terrence, was born a year later and they went on to have a daughter called Marilyn.

Sydney left the RAF shortly after the war and took a job as a gas fitter. He also worked as a milkman and a postman in later years.

Retirement came in 1989 but Sydney still worked part-time, as a lollipop man outside Trumpington Primary School.

Constance died eight years ago and Sydney spends much of his time with his son and daughter, his six grandchildren and seven great-grandchildren.

(concluding summary):

Sydney used to enjoy regular reunion dinners with his former air force colleagues but he is now the only one still alive.

He attends the city's annual Remembrance Day parade and says he will continue to do so while he is fit and healthy.

Occasionally his mind drifts back to those adrenaline-fuelled days in his Spitfire and that first dogfight when he was just 21.

"We were thankful we won the war," he added. "I didn't feel like a hero though. No-one treated me any different in the street. Everyone played their part, like Churchill said."

(stat & fact boxes):

These could be dotted around the feature to break up the words:

Battle of Britain

- July to October 1940
- Southern England & English Channel
- 544 Allied pilots killed
- 2,698 German pilots killed
- 40,000 British civilians killed

Spitfire losses in Battle of Britain

- 208 lost in combat
- 7 destroyed on the ground
- 42 lost in flying accidents

- You will notice that I have not used every note taken in the interview. There is also a chronological order I have followed after introducing Sydney and his role in the Battle of Britain. I then fill in more details about his wartime service, before rounding out his profile by mentioning his wife and what he did after the war. Compare your feature with mine and look at ways you could have improved your own piece.

2nd Feature brief:

Four of the six regular bell ringers at a village church have fallen pregnant at the same time and there is now a desperate appeal for ringers to take their place while they are on maternity leave so the bells do not fall silent. You have been tasked to interview the women, the captain of the belfry and the church rector for the basis of a feature.

Date and time:

September 17, 2015 at 4pm

Notes taken:

Helen Lester (36), of Swan Close, Oxthorpe, expecting November 14.

Sallie Gunston (28), of Handford Drive, Oxthorpe, expecting December 1.

Nicola Thorpe (27), of Swan Close, Oxthorpe, expecting November 23 (next-door neighbour of Helen).

Tamsin Newton (31), of Ontario Street, Oxthorpe, expecting next week (September 22).

All experienced bell ringers – Helen 3 years, Sallie 3 years, Nicola 4 years, Tamsin 7 years.

Tamsin took break from bell ringing in July – expecting a boy.

She said: "It's not physically hard but you are stretching up all the time and if you haven't used those muscles very often it can be tough to get used to.

"It's not possible to ring the bells right up to the birth and I will need to get fit properly and work on my stomach muscles after I have had my baby."

Sallie is a solicitor in Leicester, this will be her second child, also has son Jack (4)

She said: "There aren't that many bell ringers in the village so it is a shame we will all be out of action at the same time.

"I will miss it. It's a great social thing. We practice twice a week and have a drink in the Black Horse afterwards. We have to be available at weekends for weddings and for services."

Rector of Oxthorpe (the Rev Colin Braithwaite) – been at the church seven years.

His younger son Phillip is the only male bell ringer in the team and is the belfry captain.

The Rector said: "We are a bit short at the moment and we're always looking for ringers because some are trained and then don't stay with us or they move away from the village.

"We are going to struggle to muster the necessary six unless we can train some more up quickly.

"We don't want to disappoint people because we have a number of weddings and funerals coming up."

Takes six weeks to train a bell ringer properly – one or two training sessions a week.

Have to be available on a rota for weekends and some weekdays.

No children, need to be at least 18 and physically fit.

No upper age limit – the church used to have an 89-year-old bell ringer in 1960s.

Anyone who wants to learn can call Oxthorpe 356444 to find out more about it.

Church dates from 15ᵗʰ century – St James' Church.

Nicola and Helen became good friends after Nicola moved next door in 2010.

Having their babies nine days apart.

Nicola said: "We've told our husbands they have to train as bell ringers until we're ready to come back.

"They are not keen. We might have to work on them."

Helen said: "I would recommend people have a go at bell ringing. It's a good thing to learn and you are doing something for the community. I never thought it was something I would do but now I am really going to miss it."

Rector said: "It is quite amazing that four of the ladies are having babies around the same time. "There must be something in the water round here."

Phillip Braithwaite, belfry captain, been bell ringing there six years.

Trying to convince his wife to train as a bell ringer but she hasn't decided yet.

He said: "It might just be two of us ringing the bells at this rate. That's not possible so I don't know what we would do if we can't find replacements."

Training nights are Mondays at 7.30pm and some Thursdays (8pm), two every month.

- Once again, have a go at writing your feature based on these notes before taking a look at the specimen feature I have written at the end. Compare your efforts with my article again.

2nd Specimen feature:

(headline):

PREGNANT PAUSE FOR BABY BOOM BELLES

(standfirst):

Oxthorpe Church has a problem. Four of their six bell ringers have fallen pregnant at the same time. The race is on to find replacements soon or the village bells will fall silent. NICK RENNIE finds out more about this unusual occurrence.

(introduction):

The sound of church bells on a Sunday morning is one of the delights of living in a village but residents at Oxthorpe might be about to experience a pregnant pause in the peels where they live.

This is because not one, but four, of the bell ringers at St James' Church are expecting a baby around the same time.

They need six people to ring the bells so a desperate appeal has been sounded by the Rector, the Rev Colin Braithwaite, for new trainees to come forward while the regulars are on maternity leave.

(dynamic opening quotes):

"It is quite amazing that four of the ladies are having babies around the same time," he said.

"There must be something in the water round here."

Rev Braithwaite added: "We are going to struggle to muster the necessary six unless we can train some more up quickly.

"We don't want to disappoint people because we have a number of weddings and funerals coming up."

(flowing body of the feature):

Tamsin Newton has her baby next week so she has already stopped ringing, Helen Lester and Nicola Thorpe are due to give birth in November while Sallie Gunston has hers at the start of December.

The women all love their hobby but they say it is impossible for them to continue right up to their due dates.

Tamsin (31), of Ontario Street, who reluctantly gave up her duties in July, said: "It's not physically hard but you are stretching up all the time and if you haven't used those muscles very often it can be tough to get used to.

"It's not possible to ring the bells right up to the birth and I will need to get fit properly and work on my stomach muscles after I have had my baby."

Sallie, a 28-year-old Leicester solicitor, who lives with her husband and four-year-old son Jack in Handford Drive in the village, is concerned the church won't be able to find enough trainees to keep the bells ringing.

She said: "There aren't that many bell ringers in the village so it is a shame we will all be out of action at the same time.

"I will miss it. It's a great social thing. We practice twice a week and have a drink in the Black Horse afterwards."

The 15th century church has a peel of six bells, which are rung for weddings, funerals and fortnightly Sunday morning services.

Phillip Braithwaite, the son of the rector, is the belfry captain. He has been trying to convince his wife to train for it while the regular bell ringers are unavailable.

He said, with a chuckle: "It might just be two of us ringing the bells at this rate. That's not possible so I don't know what we would do if we can't find replacements."

(concluding summary):

Nicola (27) and 36-year-old Helen became good friends after Nicola moved next door in 2010 and was persuaded by her neighbour to have a go at bell ringing at the church.

They are both genuinely worried that there will not be enough people to ring the bells in the run-up to Christmas.

The women are having their babies nine days apart and in the meantime are trying to enlist some fresh blood for duties in the belfry.

Nicola said: "We've told our husbands they have to train as bell ringers until we're ready to come back.

"They are not keen. We might have to work on them."

Anyone who would like more information on training as a bell ringer at Oxthorpe – sessions are at 7.30pm every Monday and 8pm on two Thursdays a month – can telephone Oxthorpe 356444 to find out more about it.

(stat & fact boxes):

With this feature it might be worthwhile including some points about bell ringers although it is one of the features which could run without a stat/fact box:

Bell ringing requirements

- Must be aged at least 18
- No upper age limit
- Must be physically fit
- Available on a rota at weekends

- You will notice once again that I didn't use every note taken in the interview. This type of feature is more of a challenge, particularly when you are learning to be a journalist, because there are multiple people to interview. It's important to take clear notes and not to mix up any of the people involved. This is an offbeat feature where you can inject a bit of humour, as you can see with the heading and some of the quotes. These features work well because they have a real human element to them and they touch on the lives of real people.

You should now be able to write really good features if you have followed the advice in this chapter and they will get better the more you write.

Next we will look at how journalists use social media, not only to promote their news stories but also to source new ones.

CHAPTER 7

HOW YOU CAN USE SOCIAL MEDIA AS A JOURNALIST

CHAPTER 7: How you can use social media as a journalist

This is an exciting time to work as a journalist because of the increasing importance of digital publishing.

When I started out in the industry the only product we produced was a printed newspaper.

Readers had to wait until Thursday to get their weekly diet of news, features and sport.

But every news outlet now is effectively a 24/7 daily media operation, where breaking stories have to go on the website as soon as you can write them.

Reporters post on social media live from incidents and meetings so readers (and online followers) can get a real time update.

So it is absolutely essential that you familiarise yourself with social media because it is another vitally important channel to report the news on.

Why then do people bother to continue buying the newspaper, I hear you ask?

Well, there are readers who aren't tech-savvy and generations of older people who still prefer the feel of a physical newspaper.

But, equally, there are plenty of people who do use social media and who would rather receive their news in a digital format, either via a link on Twitter or Facebook, for example, or through the publication's website.

The value of all this is that online traffic to the website of a newspaper or broadcaster increases and so effectively does the value of advertising revenue on the site.

At a time when the money raised through the sale of space for adverts in the printed issue has fallen dramatically this is an important development.

So it is critical that journalists use social media to regularly post good content or links to interesting stories and features throughout the day.

Certain channels work very well for news outlets and in this chapter I will outline how you can do this effectively as a journalist with a newspaper or a broadcast company.

6 USEFUL SOCIAL MEDIA CHANNELS FOR JOURNALISTS

1 Twitter

There are currently around 10 million users of Twitter in the UK and 280 million worldwide.

The value of this channel to a journalist is that you can post short sharp content (no more than 140 characters) to flag up a breaking story with a link to your website.

It's great for generating online traffic for newspapers and for tasting articles which readers can read in greater depth in the latest printed issue of the paper.

A reporter can Tweet the verdict in an important court case live from the hearing or they can inform people about the outcome of a contentious planning application seconds after it is known.

Journalists can also pick up stories on their patch by monitoring posts by people they follow in their community or by searching for Tweets about their town and villages and the people and organisations in them.

2 Facebook

More than a third of people in the UK are now on Facebook and four out of five users in this country access their account via a mobile device, such as a tablet computer or a mobile phone.

So it is a great place to reach potential readers or listeners at any time of the day.

You can post news stories and features with images with the aim of getting people in the patch you cover to share the content with their friends.

It's akin to them passing a friend or relative a copy of your newspaper for them to read or handing over their headphones so they can listen to your radio station's news bulletins.

Where this scores over Twitter is that you can go into more detail with an article and you can also prompt feedback and comments which might also move the story on and give you another angle.

3 You Tube

By setting up a channel on this platform newspapers can effectively turn themselves into broadcasters as well.

They can post videos of a Royal visit to the town, for example, or an interview with the Mayor or the local football club's new signing.

Some newspapers also produce a news bulletin of stories which have broken that day, interspersed with video footage of events.

Most mobile phones have the capacity these days to shoot high quality videos if you don't have a camcorder available in the office and it is relatively simple to edit the film.

You can also include links to the story on the news outlet's website and because You Tube is owned by Google this will help with ranking the article highly on internet search pages.

4 Instagram

Newspapers take a rich variety of photographs during a working week and this channel gives you the ideal place to showcase them.

It's also a great account for posting images which don't make the print issue or the website – snaps taken by reporters on their mobile phones when a celebrity is opening a new store, perhaps, or when business people are attending an awards night.

It's a great way of engaging with the community by following local people, commenting on their image posts and getting them to comment on yours.

The channel can also be used to drive sales of photographs by including contact details for reception staff or photographers.

Instagram is becoming more and more relevant and now has more active users than Twitter - 300 million worldwide at the time of going to press.

5 Periscope

This is a new livestreaming app which media organisations quickly picked up as a way of making short video films on mobile phones and tablet computers.

Journalists can report live from an incident or they can give their audience an insight into what it is like to be at a big event or an interesting location.

TV reporters used it to record footage back stage at the 2015 General Election leadership debates.

Where it also scores is the geolocation feature which enables journalists to follow others on Periscope by searching for streams taken at specific locations.

So reporters can instantly pick up people who might have witnessed an accident or a big public protest, for example, and use their comments in their story.

6 LinkedIn

Journalists need to have a profile on this professional social networking site, to help them do their job more effectively but also to source their next career move.

By making connections with influential people on your patch you are building relationships which should bear fruit in the form of tip-offs for stories and quotes for your articles.

By following the major employers in the territory you cover you'll get first wind of interesting developments, such as new jobs being created, jobs being lost or new products and services launched.

It's well worthwhile linking with other journalists, even those working for rival outlets, and to take part in journalism discussion forums.

You will hear about vacancies which might interest you when you're ready to move on because many job adverts are now posted on LinkedIn.

SETTING UP YOUR OWN SOCIAL MEDIA PROFILE

The importance of social media to the work journalists do is illustrated by a recent study which found that 51 per cent of them felt they couldn't do their job without access to the likes of Twitter and Facebook.

The Global Social Journalism Study, by Cision, also indicated that two-thirds of journalists spent up to two hours a day on social media in the course of their working day.

This was a poll of 3,000 journalists in the UK, the US, Europe and Australia so the sample was not insignificant.

It is clear that the modern journalist has to be armed with a mobile device which is permanently connected to the internet, whether that is a smartphone or a tablet computer.

And they also need to make use of apps for the various social media feeds so they can post updates or source breaking news wherever they are.

Twitter, if used correctly, can produce a rolling timeline of potential news items in the form of Tweets from organisations and individuals with an influence in the patch or the industry that you cover.

Most news organisations encourage individual journalists to set up their own Twitter account so they can build relationships with useful contacts and the general readership.

If you are setting yours up from scratch then my advice would be to make sure you include a good recent image of yourself and a professional profile biography.

It is important that you are visible in the community and for others to see the human face of the news outlet you represent.

If you leave the photograph element blank on Twitter the evidence is that far fewer people will take the trouble to follow you.

Readers like to see the person behind the stories in their local paper or the newsreader on their favourite radio station.

If your Twitter page doubles as both your work and personal account then it is advisable to include the phrase 'these are my thoughts and not those of my employer' to cover yourself, for example, when you've praised your beloved football team or criticised customer service at a shop you've bought something from.

It's worthwhile setting up a personal LinkedIn page too, particularly if you work on stories which relate to business, education, local government and health issues.

This will enable you to make connections with the influential players in these sectors and build a relationship and a measure of trust with these individuals.

You will also become aware of developments in their working lives which could be potential news stories for you to cover.

If you are out and about a lot within your working day you should also look to set up personal accounts for Instagram, to share images from your various assignments, and Periscope, to provide a live video feed to elements of your working day.

Facebook and You Tube accounts work better as company accounts for the overall news outlet rather than for individual journalists.

We will look at these platforms in more detail later in this chapter.

Top tips on how journalists can use social networking effectively

Since early 2014, more people have been accessing the internet via mobile devices than via personal desktop computers with a fixed connection.

What this means for journalists is that you can reach a significant proportion of readers, listeners and viewers at any time of the day on their smartphones and tablets.

You will constantly be updating your news outlet's website, of course, with breaking news and updates to other stories.

But to drive online traffic to your site you need to harness the power of social media by building communities of followers and sharing links to your stories and features in your posts.

Here are some top tips on how to do just that.

1 Build a relevant community of connections

The first step to doing this is to make a list of all the important individuals and organisations on the patch or in the industry that you cover.

Then check to see if they have a Twitter page, either through the site's 'search' feature or their relevant website, and simply follow them.

Some will follow you back but if a key person or organisation doesn't then send them a Tweet, including their Twitter username, with a short message saying hello and asking if they would like to connect.

Now, the way to ensure these people keeping following you is to post regular interesting comment.

Not just links to stories you have written but insights into your working day, when you are covering an interesting assignment, for example, or you're at an event where you can share a good image.

Personal stuff works too because it shows more of your personality and your interests and followers will warm to that.

Don't be shy about praising others on Twitter. If you've eaten a meal at a local restaurant or had great service from the council then give them a mention. Everyone likes complements and a positive reaction to you can only be a good thing on social media.

LinkedIn is more of a closed shop in terms of social networks. You can only connect with others if both parties agree.

The best way to build your LinkedIn profile is to connect with relevant people when you deal with them, either face-to-face, on the phone or by email.

Ask them if they are on the social network and, if they are, then ask if they would like to connect. It's effectively like swapping business cards.

Once again you will need to post regular updates on LinkedIn to keep your account fresh and keep connections interested.

Make sure your profile is up-to-date and that there are plenty of contact details for people to get in touch in the event that they want to volunteer information for a story or a tip-off for one.

With any social media channel, and this includes Instagram and Periscope, it is important that you include a photo of yourself and a potted profile. You need to make people aware that you are a journalist and if you use social networks properly you can develop really effective channels of communication with relevant sources.

2 Schedule your posts

One of the biggest mistakes people make on social media is to overload your audience with messages.

It's a bit like someone talking incessantly to you. Eventually you ask them to stop or you walk away.

There is a need to post regular content and over a working day you will find it is fairly easy to space out Tweets or Facebook posts, for example.

But what if you are busy in court for days on end or you are at an event with no online connection or on holiday?

You want to post fresh material but you don't want to send them all together so that you clog up the timelines of followers.

The answer is to use a free social media scheduling tool, such as Hootsuite.

This allows you to type a series of Tweets for the coming day or week and stagger them to be posted at various times.

The advantage is that your followers will get a steady stream of fresh content, keeping your profile high while you are incapacitated.

The main disadvantage is that you would be unable to respond immediately if someone comments on one of these posts so it is wise to steer clear of content for which people might require an instant answer.

A tool like Hootsuite allows you to schedule posts on any social media channel you operate on.

It also gives you a clear view on the analytics – there are columns showing posts which have been retweeted and shared and those which have been favourited or liked. This will give you an indication on which of your posts and, effectively, which of your stories are creating a buzz online.

3 Use hashtags

If you want your posts on platforms like Twitter and Instagram to have the widest possible audience then you need to make good use of the # symbol, known in the Twitterverse as the hashtag.

This will allow other users of Twitter to find your posts and, most importantly, links to news stories on your outlet's website.

For example, if you are writing about the National Space Centre in Leicester you will need to include the hashtags #space and #Leicester as well as the centre's username, @spacecentre, in your Tweet.

Users will be searching for specific terms on Twitter and by using these hashtags your post will be seen by those looking for content about space and about Leicester, even if those people don't actively follow your account.

Hashtags can also be useful if you are looking for witnesses to an event or people you want to quote or interview in a story.

You can ask people to use a specific hashtag to get involved in a debate on a particular issue.

For instance, if you are writing an article about a tram strike in Manchester for the Manchester Evening News (MEN) you could ask for comments using the hashtag #TramStrikeMEN.

You should aim to use the Twitter username of the person or the organisation you are posting about on social media since they will also be aware of the content and may also add something to the debate or move your story on to another angle.

4 Use the 'search' feature regularly

On your Twitter page you will see a search bar which enables you to find content you are interested in.

You can either search for phrases, usernames or hashtags. This is a really useful feature if you are short of news or you are looking for issues which are creating a buzz in your patch.

Many major news stories have actually broken on Twitter through Tweets by members of the public before journalists have been aware of what was happening.

The 2013 Boston Marathon bombing in the United States and the plane crashing into the Hudson River in New York in 2009 were both first mentioned by Tweeters who saw it happen.

Countless other stories – both significant global occurrences and those of interest to a more local audience – have had their first airing on social media.

So it is worthwhile performing a Twitter search on the town, county or region you cover.

The search function can also be used as extra research on a story you are working on. You can pick up posts which change the angle of your article or you may find someone you can potentially quote.

I wrote a story recently about an earthquake which hit the town of Melton Mowbray in Leicestershire.

By searching for 'earthquake Melton Mowbray' I discovered several posts by people who experienced the unusual happening. I was able to use some of the Tweets in my story to add colour to the piece.

5 Post images or videos

Recent research (Media Blog) has shown that Tweets which include images get 35 per cent more retweets than those which don't have any.

The value of the retweet is that people are effectively endorsing your content and sharing it with their followings. And ultimately it will be seen by a greater audience.

The same is true of Facebook. A study of posts in 2014 (eMarketer) showed that of those that were shared, 87 per cent had images in them.

The importance of photographs on social media is illustrated by the increasing popularity of Instagram, which now has more active users than Twitter.

So it is well worthwhile posting images when you are out reporting at events or interviewing people or including a photo taken by your news outlet's photographer.

Videos also get plenty of shares but it's important they are short – no longer than 90 seconds.

This is because people browsing online have very low attention span thresholds.

They will not watch to the end of your film if it drags on but if it is interesting and concise it will likely be shared.

How news outlets use social media channels successfully

Until the last decade or so the only interaction newspapers had with their readers was via the letters page.

And this was a strictly controlled process with editors deciding which correspondence they printed in each issue and also taking the opportunity to edit the content.

Now, of course, social networking allows people to comment on stories as soon as they appear, either online or in print.

This is also the case with radio and TV news and sports broadcasters, who now have the opportunity to weave the social media posts of listeners and viewers into their coverage.

Here are some of the ways news outlets harness the power of social media to enhance their output.

Obtaining feedback on their coverage

Newspapers keep an eye on the analytics for their social media channels to see which stories are being shared or commented on the most.

This is important intelligence when it comes to deciding news agendas because it can sometimes yield surprising results.

Offbeat stories can often be the most popular with readers so it is important to reflect this in the paper in terms of placing them nearer the front rather than burying them in the middle pages.

An article referring to a popular celebrity or brand often generates the biggest buzz online, particularly if they are mentioned in the headlines to ensure they feature high in the Google search rankings.

Stories featuring good images or interesting videos will also be popular with an online audience.

Social posts are also important for feedback because they can inform journalists if there are inaccuracies in their copy or if they have missed a more interesting angle to the story.

Seeking sources

When a major incident has happened there will often be a series of Tweets, Facebook posts and Instagram images from the scene.

This provides instant material for journalists looking for immediate witnesses they can quote in their story, assuming they are not reporting live at the location of course.

This is public content which can be instantly accessed to provide a bit of colour to the piece.

On occasions, if it is a sensitive issue for example, then a decision might be taken not to use the material.

Social media can also be used to identify contributors to a topical story. A Tweet can be sent out or a Facebook post asking for people to get in touch who have used a service which has been axed or who have an interest in a contentious planning application.

Researching stories

When you are reporting about an individual or an organisation you can often glean useful information from their social media posts.

And by performing a search on Twitter it is also possible to see a timeline of posts around a specific incident or issue to get an understanding of it before you report on it.

Twitter, Facebook or LinkedIn also act as additional channels to make contact with someone if you don't have a telephone number or an email address for them.

I recall writing an article about a fatal car crash. The police released the name of the victim but we could not find any phone numbers for the family.

A quick search on Facebook gave us an opportunity to contact family members respectfully to ask if they would like us to publish a tribute to the woman who had sadly died.

They gave us information about her life and also allowed us to use a treasured image which had been posted on her Facebook page.

Driving online traffic to the outlet's official website

Facebook can be used as an extra website for a newspaper or broadcaster with the opportunity to publish articles and images, as well as links to radio or television coverage.

Some outlets prefer to taste stories on social media and include a link to a fuller version on the website or direct them to the printed publication.

Social sites can also provide another place for contact details for the websites and telephone and email details for individual journalists.

More and more people use Facebook and You Tube to search for content as opposed to using Google or another search engine.

So it is well worthwhile posting regular interesting content on these channels to ensure there is plenty of traffic being directed to the news outlet's website.

Building relationships with contacts

Social media platforms allow journalists to foster strong working relationships with relevant individuals and organisations.

Local newspapers should follow Twitter accounts on their patch and regularly interact with them.

This doesn't mean constantly plugging stories but commenting on the activities or services other businesses in their locality are involved with.

Cultivating online connections will make them much more likely to contact you if they have something newsworthy to tell you and it will also reflect a positive reputation for the news outlet.

As mentioned before, social channels also give journalists another way to communicate with potential sources if they can't be reached by telephone or email.

To help you process some of the points made in this chapter, here is a quick checklist of things you should be doing on social media when you are working as a journalist:

- Make sure you include a profile photograph of yourself on your social media accounts and a biography describing which media outlet you work for

- Make connections with relevant organisations and people on your patch and build relationships and a sense of trust by interacting with them

- Post links to stories and updated articles to drive online traffic to your website

- Use the Twitter search feature to look for issues and topics important to people who live on your patch

- Reporters should set up their own Twitter, Instagram, LinkedIn and Periscope accounts and post regular, fresh content as well as links to stories (Facebook and You Tube pages should represent the media organisation as a whole)

- Post photographs and short videos because they tend to be shared by more people than normal posts

- Act respectfully and professionally when you are responding to comments by readers on something you have posted on social media

- Use relevant hashtags when posting on Twitter and Instagram to help people search for your content

- Don't overload the timelines of followers by posting too regularly – space it out during the day or schedule it using a free tool such as Hootsuite

- Follow rival news organisations to pick up potential stories and follow-ups

- Do online searches for social media profiles for sources for stories or other people involved in your reports when you have no other contact details

- Make connections on LinkedIn with relevant individuals on your patch and other journalists

So, start developing your personal online social profile using the advice in this chapter so you can hit the ground running when you start working as a journalist.

Next, we will look at the role of today's multi-media journalists, where reporters are expected to take photographs with the office camera or their mobile phone to run alongside the articles they write.

You will find out how best to compose photographs for use in a newspaper or on a news organisation's website and what you can and can't photograph as a journalist.

CHAPTER 8

TAKING PHOTOGRAPHS AND TIPS FOR PHOTOJOURNALISTS

CHAPTER 8: Taking photographs and tips for photojournalists

The days of newspaper and broadcast reporters heading off on assignments armed just with a notebook and pen are long gone.

These days you need to also have with you either a mobile phone capable of taking good quality photographs or the office compact digital camera.

And in some instances you may even be asked to take along a camcorder to record an event for posting footage on your outlet's website and social media channels.

Of course, for some news and sports stories you will be accompanied by an in-house or freelance photographer so you will only have to concentrate on making accurate notes and taking down quotes.

But newsrooms and sports desks operate with fewer resources and there is an increasing requirement for reporters to be multi-media journalists, capable of grabbing a quote from an important source, taking their photograph and even videoing the interview.

It can be quite a juggling act preparing all the various devices while also making sure you have a clear note of everything in case the technology lets you down. And it occasionally does!

In this chapter we will explore what makes a good photograph for a news organisation and enable you to shoot pictures which can be displayed on the front page of a newspaper or alongside a prominent story on an outlet's website.

I will also include some examples of good and bad photographs and explain why they are so.

Some readers of this book will be talented photographers in their own right and they may be looking at a career as a photojournalist.

I have been asked several times how to get into this area of the industry so we will end the chapter by establishing a few pointers on how to do just that.

7 TOP TIPS FOR SHOOTING THE PERFECT PRESS PHOTOGRAPH

1 Make sure it is a high enough resolution

This is, perhaps, the most important thing to remember because if the image is not a big enough file size it can't be used in a printed newspaper.

There are two measurements of a digital photograph which will tell you if it is a high enough resolution for a print title.

If you want to use the picture big on a page – with a dramatic front page splash, for example, or to run with a full-page feature - then it should ideally be at least 1mb (megabyte) and preferably 2mb.

If the photo is to go with a lesser story, or 'downpage' article as they are referred to in the industry, then 80 to 100kb (kilobytes) will suffice.

Alternatively, you can check resolution via the dpi (Dots Per Inch) measurement. For print use, you are looking at images of a minimum of 150dpi and preferably 300dpi.

When you plan to use images on a website or on social media you can get away with a much lower resolution.

In this case, anything above 25kb will be sufficient although if you want to display it bigger on your site then 60kb or higher is the figure to look for. In terms of dpi, you will need around 72 for website images.

Of course, if the photo is out of focus, over-exposed (too light) or under-exposed (too dark) then none of the above measures are important because it won't be good enough to use in print or online.

A good tip here is to try to take photographs outside, if at all possible, because the natural light will improve quality as opposed to shooting indoors where artificial room lighting can spoil the picture.

And don't face the sun while taking pictures. Try to position yourself so the sun is behind you, if it is shining brightly that day.

2 Include relevant props

This is a nice trick press photographers use to make their pictures more interesting. Sometimes it is obvious. If someone has won a medal or they are showing off a prize-winning vegetable then it makes sense to snap them holding those objects.

But what if the subject of a story has been accepted on a TV cooking show, such as *Masterchef* or *The Great British Bake Off?*

There are no images yet of them on set at the show but don't just settle for a bland 'head and shoulders' photo. Get them dressed in a kitchen apron holding a saucepan or a carving knife.

That kind of photograph is much more likely to draw the reader's eye and influence them to read your story.

I remember writing a piece about a middle-aged woman who won a part in a local operatic society show when her only experience was singing to herself in the bath.

The photographer mocked up a shot – preserving her modesty with a strapless swimsuit - with her laying back in her bath singing away with a shower cap on her head.

There is a thin line, however, between illustrating a story with a prop in a humorous or striking way and going over the top to the point of absurdity.

For instance, if a lottery jackpot winner has been told on the phone that he has won a fortune it is not a good idea to mock up a picture of them holding the telephone receiver with a look of incredulity on his face.

In this case you are better off handing him a wad of money and getting him to throw the bank notes in the air or just holding them with a jubilant expression.

When using props in a photograph an important point to remember is to make sure your subject is holding them up prominently.

So a competition winner should be photographed holding their prize up to the camera, to make it stand out in the image and also to allow the picture to be used lengthways (landscape) or upright (portrait) on a print or web page.

Take a look at national newspapers during the Olympic Games and you will see athletes holding their medals just below the chin or to the side of their heads and sometimes biting them.

They are clearly much more dynamic and interesting images than if they were pictured simply standing there with the medal dangling down at their waist.

One prop which is now frowned upon by most editors is the cheque. Newspapers used to be full of photos of cheque presentations following charity fundraisers or grants being awarded for community projects but they are now considered to be too dull to use.

They often featured huge cheques with the amount written on them or tiny cheques which were barely visible.

You will need to check with your editor but the chances are that they will have banned the use of cheques in photographs so a simple hand shake or the relevant parties with an alternative prop will need to be snapped instead.

3 Avoid dead space

Space is at a premium in newspapers so the photographs need to be composed in such a way that all of the areas of the image are worthwhile using.

What do we mean by 'dead space'? It basically refers to a portion of a photo which serves no purpose and which essentially wastes space.

This might be the trousers and shoes in a line-up of members of a rotary club toasting their latest fundraising achievement – the image only needs to contain their bodies above the waist holding up a glass of whatever alcohol is being drunk.

In sports team photos, team members should be arranged in distinct equal rows with no big gaps between each person.

If one of the players is standing or sitting on the end of a line, a distance away from their team-mates, there is dead space in the picture and it is not aesthetically pleasing to the eye either.

A school picture showing a teacher towering over two pupils will also contain a measure of dead space (the area above the children's heads) so it would be better to ask the teacher to crouch down so they are nearer the pupils to produce a much better balanced photo.

4 Shoot against a suitable background

Readers of newspapers I have worked on have often sent in good quality photographs of people but the backdrop is a bland brick wall.

Other snaps have been taken with rubbish bins in the background or signs advertising public toilets clearly visible.

The end result is that you end up with a dull photograph with intrusive elements which draw the reader's eye away from the subject of the image.

The same is true if you have people in the background who are unconnected with the story you are trying to illustrate.

And if these interlopers, or photo-bombers as they are now called, are pulling a face or making an unfortunate gesture then the picture is unusable anyway.

Be on the lookout for intrusive elements in the background which can also distort your picture, such as a tree or plant which appears to grow out of someone's head when you finally get to see it later on your computer screen.

A good tip when you are taking a head and shoulders of someone or a group shot outside the office is to take it with a neutral street scene behind them.

That way the background is sufficiently interesting and not distracting enough to prevent your subjects standing out.

Parkland and flowers also provide decent backdrops, as do coastlines if you are lucky enough to be snapping away at the seaside.

5 Move up close for head and shoulders pictures

These are staple images for newspapers and broadcasters. When new councillors are elected your editor will want portrait photographs of each of them and before a new football or cricket season the sports editor will request head shots of all the players individually.

The advantage of these pictures is they can be dropped into a story or match report to break up the words.

A good tip is to take two versions of each person – a smiling one and a more serious snap – so the editor has an option to use them with light-hearted and serious stories.

It may sound obvious but the main thing with these pictures is to get up close to the subject.

They will only be used to show a person's face and their shoulders and if you stand too far back it won't be possible to use the image as a head shot since the resolution drops appreciably the more you focus in on it on a computer screen.

In some head and shoulders photos I have seen the subject is standing awkwardly, invariably because people never know what to do with their arms.

A press photographer I used to work with always used a little trick of getting the subject to stand sideways, but looking straight at the camera, with their arms crossed.

It's a very relaxed pose which puts the subject at ease and it also enables the picture to be used deeper on a page if there is more space available.

6 Crop some images to improve composition

The chances are that you won't capture the perfect shot when you are out on an assignment.

But all is not lost. A good crop can improve your picture immeasurably if you have access to software such as *Photoshop* or *Paint* or a free online image editor such as *Pixlr*.

You can crop out dead space or distracting background images and also lighten or darken the picture.

Be aware, though, that the more you crop your photo the smaller the resolution will be.

When you crop the image also make sure you save it under a different name from the original so you can always go back to it if required.

7 Take names for captions

More arguments have been caused between editors and photographers down the years because there are no names to go with the picture than any other issue.

This is sometimes down to the snapper not having enough time to take the names, because a sports match was due to start or the subjects had to dash off.

But occasionally it is down purely to laziness. So get into the mindset of taking names for your photographs.

Readers will identify people they know or have heard about when a caption is included so it adds another important element of interest to the photograph and the associated story.

As we touched on earlier in this book, spelling the names correctly is essential. Make a clear note of the names and get subjects to spell their names out for you, whether they are familiar or not.

If you are taking photographs for stories involving children then you MUST seek the permission of parents, guardians or teachers.

If it means leaving children out of a group line-up when the parents have requested they are not identified then you must do so.

Many schools canvas parents before the start of each school year to ask if they would object to their children being in photographs and this has made the job of the press that much easier.

The same guidelines apply when you are taking photographs in a swimming pool – be aware of any children in the background for whom you haven't obtained the necessary clearance.

EXAMPLES OF GOOD AND BAD PRESS PHOTOGRAPHS

Image 1 BAD picture:

This photo features one of the worst possible backgrounds for a press picture – a dreary brick wall.

The purpose of the image is to show a woman celebrating with the medals she has won but they are held low down and there is no expression on her face.

The picture is very unlikely to draw a reader in to read the story unless they know the lady personally.

Image 1 GOOD picture:

Here the medals are held high in the foreground and close to the face. There is also a much more pleasing floral background in the garden and the lady is smiling.

Readers are much more likely to engage with this image and it can also be used as a tighter shot by cropping the background out if space is at a premium on the page.

Image 2 BAD picture:

There are a multitude of things wrong with this as a press image, which you should be able to instantly identify.

The background is dull, particularly the washing line and the women are standing too far apart as though they are not willing participants. The poppy, which was one of those in the 2014 Tower of London remembrance display, should be the centre of attention but it is clutched low and not at all prominently.

Image 2 GOOD picture:

This is much better. The women are closer together and the poppy is being held high and in the centre of the image.

The background is also much more interesting with flowers, the tops of neighbouring properties and the skyline all visible instead of the washing line.

It can also be cropped tighter if required.

Image 3 BAD picture:

This picture was taken at the Burghley Horse Trials in Lincolnshire and shows top eventer William Fox-Pitt having to stop briefly during his cross country ride.

The negative points with this one are that the rider and horse both have their backs to the camera and the background is largely an uninteresting line of trees. It's a bland photo which doesn't really tell us anything about what is going on.

Image 3 GOOD picture:

This is a much better photo of Fox-Pitt at the event which would be worthy of using as a main image on a page or accompanying an online report of the competition.

Both rider and horse are facing the camera, you can see people in the crowd watching on and in the far background is the Burghley House stately home.

The rider is also seen looking ahead to check if he can continue his round, which adds a nice 'active' feel to the image.

Image 4 GOOD picture:

The boy is captured here taking part in a drumming workshop at a village festival. He is photographed with a puppeteer and it works well as a tight shot with a good background showing some of the other drummers in action.

Image 5 GOOD picture:

This is a good example of how to set up a photo when you have two subjects and no props.

The boxer on the left has just signed a deal with the promoter on the right so they were posed shaking hands as well as doing something positive and dynamic with their other hands.

It's a much more pleasing image than if the photograph had just shown them standing side-by-side facing the camera.

HOW TO SET YOURSELF UP AS A PHOTOJOURNALIST

So, you see yourself as a bit of an all-rounder. You can write but you are also a dab hand behind the lens.

With these skills you will undoubtedly be a big asset as a multi-media journalist in a modern day news organisation but you could also carve out a very good career for yourself as a freelance photojournalist.

There is a need to turn around news stories rapidly with space on websites as well as print titles to fill 24/7.

And if you can provide the words and a great image in one package your services will be in great demand with the bigger news outlets and magazines.

Ultimately you could end up being posted to glamorous travel locations abroad, you might be assigned to following candidates around the country during a General Election or you may even be embedded with troops in a war zone if you are brave enough to take that on.

But how do you get yourself known as a photojournalist? Here are a few pointers on how you can make editors aware of your abilities.

1 Build a portfolio of your published work

You need to convince editors about the quality of your photographs and stories so get out and about and start reporting and snapping away.

Go to community events, sports matches or royal visits, for example, and take a variety of pictures to send to news organisations.

Write stories to go with your photos and when they are published make sure you get hold of a copy and an online link if they appear on a website.

As we have mentioned before in this book, fewer newspapers employ an in-house photographer these days and they rely on freelancers and pictures taken by reporters and readers.

Local newspapers won't pay for your work unless it is a unique, vitally-important story but regional and national titles will.

The important thing when you are starting out, though, is to build your reputation so you have collateral in the shape of a collection of quality press clippings to back up the service you are offering.

A good portfolio will eventually lead to editors relying on you to bring regular content in and they will pay a retainer fee for supplying it.

2 Monitor the news agenda

Be aware of what is happening and what is about to happen. You need to be there when a big story is about to break because the onus is on you to capture images as well as write a report.

Draft out a calendar of upcoming events – of national as well as regional importance – so you can be available on the day and ensure you have press accreditation if any is needed.

Read the national newspapers as well as the local and regional ones so you are aware of what is topical.

And listen to radio and television news and sports bulletins to keep up with stories which are leading the news agenda.

When you are on an assignment look for something different. An alternative angle or an eye-catching image can make all the difference to an editor who is considering whether to use your work or not.

3 File your images and copy as quickly as possible

This is vital, particularly when you are sending content in to national newspapers and magazines which will be inundated by material on the same subject from other freelancers.

You will need to have a mobile device with a good internet connection in order to email photographs and copy from out in the field.

News organisations, whether they are nationals or small local weeklies, will want the material as quickly as possible so they can post it online.

They may also be on deadline too and it is vital, of course, that you are aware of when the publication in question goes to press.

If the content is too late you may well have missed out on them using it at all because someone has got there before you or the story becomes dated.

4 Pitch your work professionally

You need to be aware of exactly what the editor wants from a job. This means getting in contact with them beforehand, if there is time to do so, and also researching the title to see how they cover similar stories and what space they allocate to them.

Send an email offering your services, ask if the title is interested in what you are reporting on and, if so, how many images they want.

It's a good idea to refer to a previous article they have carried on the same subject or issue so the editor is aware you have taken a real interest in their publication.

If you are pitching content retrospectively make sure you send a limited number of photos to the newspaper or magazine – too many may clog up an email inbox which won't help your chances of being published.

Include a breakdown of your fee – assuming you are not pitching to a local weekly – and it might be worth stating that it is negotiable. This is because when you are starting out your main aim is to get material published. If you can build a good reputation the financial rewards will follow.

5 Take your camera everywhere you go

Make sure your camera is at least in the boot of your car even when you are out shopping or visiting relatives or friends.

You never know when you will find yourself in the middle of, or close to, a major news event.

And if it is particularly big it could make your reputation as a photojournalist. You will kick yourself if your lens is back at home when you are on the spot when a bus crashes into a bridge or public disorder breaks out at a demonstration.

Of course, you may well have your mobile phone with you. And in many cases you can take perfectly good images with it but if a major story is breaking you want to have your very best equipment close at hand.

You should now be in a position, if you have taken everything on board in this chapter, to be able to shoot quality press photographs good enough to use in printed newspapers and on the websites of news organisations.

Next we will look at how you can get a toe in the door in the industry by setting up an internship or period of work experience with a newspaper or broadcaster.

The chapter will also show you how to collate a portfolio of work which can be used to secure you a job interview and, ultimately, help you get that job you want in the industry.

CHAPTER 9

WORK EXPERIENCE AND BUILDING A PRESS PORTFOLIO

CHAPTER 9: Work experience and building a press portfolio

So you've read this far in the book and you will probably now be eager to start working towards that dream career in journalism.

I will assume that you have no experience of working in the industry.

If you've taken on board the tips and advice in the preceding chapters it is time to put what you've learned into practice.

Some of you reading this book will have enrolled on a journalism degree at a university or a training course with the National Council for the Training of Journalists (NCTJ).

Others will be aiming to take up a trainee position with a newspaper, a radio station or a television news outlet without having been trained.

But there are two things everyone can start doing right away.

The first is to seek work experience, preferably with your local newspaper.

And the second is to actually start reporting on events in your community and send them to the relevant media for possible publication.

You need to build a portfolio of work to show how committed you are to a job in journalism.

And a sure fire way of achieving this is to get some of your work published.

Anyone who has press clippings to show an editor will have a great chance of getting a job, whether that is following a period of training or as a fresh-faced rookie.

If you manage to get anything used by a newspaper or magazine then make sure you get a copy of it, either an online link to it or the printed version, and preferably both.

Keep a record of every press article you get into print and display them professionally in a binder or a good quality photograph album.

You will be amazed at the kudos this will give you when you are pitching your services to journalists.

THREE TOP TIPS TO SECURE WORK EXPERIENCE IN THE MEDIA

1 Demonstrate a commitment to a career as a journalist

Without doing this your application will be rejected. Newspapers and broadcasters get inundated with requests to do work placements with them.

Some young people see journalism as a glamorous career and more exciting than, say, a job with a supermarket's marketing department or an insurance broker's administration centre.

But if you don't show a keen interest in the role from the start then an editor won't consider you.

The process should start with a letter of application, rather than an email, which will show you've taken time to apply.

Find out who you should address the letter to – it will likely be the editor, the deputy editor or news editor – and spell their name correctly.

You should be able to find this information in the newspaper itself or on the website of the media title or broadcaster.

Tell them what your future plans are to secure a career in the industry, whether that involves training, study or an internship.

And also let them know why you are suited to the role and what value you can add while you are working for them.

In the challenging economic climate of recent years news teams are shrinking so any help journalists can get in terms of writing articles, proof-reading or taking photographs will be appreciated.

2 Research the news outlet you are applying to

This is also crucial. You must read back copies of the newspaper or magazine you want work experience with.

Buy the latest copy and read it cover to cover. Then go to the library and look at past issues. Make a note of lead stories, particularly front page splashes.

Jot down the different sections in the publication, such as entertainment, nostalgia and special features.

If you have an interest in any of these, or an inside knowledge, then you can volunteer your services to work on those stories.

Look at the balance of articles, how many are hard news, features, picture stories or short news in briefs (or NIBS as they are known).

Make a note of what tone the newspaper or magazine is written in. In simple terms, is it conservative with a small 'c' or is it hard hitting and aggressive on local issues?

Do some research on the history of the publication and what geographical areas it covers.

This is particularly important in local newspapers because they will not cover news outside their patch unless there is a strong link to a local individual or organisation.

The same goes for radio news work experience. Listen to their broadcasts, get a feel for the subject matter they cover and whether they report live or just via studio bulletins.

3 Ask perceptive questions at the interview

If you've considered the first two top tips here then the third should be easy. The editor or news editor will ask you to tell them about yourself right at the beginning of your interview.

Explain why you want to work there and demonstrate your passion for a career in the industry.

Talk about the newspaper and highlight articles which interested you in particular.

Tell them about your own interests and how that knowledge can be of use if you are taken on for a placement.

There will doubtless be a chance for you to ask questions. Don't ever say something along the lines of 'no, I think we've covered everything'.

Ask about what kind of role you would play at the newspaper, the magazine or on the radio station.

Ask whether you will get the chance to shadow a reporter or a photographer and what kind of feedback you will get from journalists.

And also make it clear that you would like experience of writing content for the publication so you have clippings for your portfolio to help your career develop.

Don't be afraid to ask questions. It can only make a positive impression when you show an interest in working for someone and you can demonstrate that you've thought deeply about it.

THREE KEY WAYS YOU CAN BUILD YOUR OWN PRESS PORTFOLIO CLIPPINGS

1 Report on a community event

There are dozens of local happenings in the town or village where you live which would make great copy for your local paper.

Family fun days, fetes, beer festivals, music festivals, charity fundraisers, school sports days. The list is endless. Local papers or radio stations don't have the manpower to report on all of them so they would be grateful to you if you did the job for them.

Get hold of the organiser to get a rundown of all the activities taking place and get a quote or two off them.

Find out if the event is raising money for a charity or a local organisation.

And take photographs because it is a fair bet that the local media will not have the resources to take their own.

More local newspapers are staffed by freelance photographers rather than in-house ones and they tend to ask people who run these events to take their own and email them in.

You don't need a fancy camera, either. Most mobile phones can take good quality images which are more than good enough for use in a publication.

If you do take photographs, record the names of people in them and make sure the spellings are correct. Tell them, of course, that your intentions are to send them to the local media, especially when children are in the pictures. You should also ask permission of their parents as well.

2 Interview an interesting local character

In every community there are lots of people who do unusual jobs or who have achieved something special.

There will be older people who may have given distinguished service in the military, for example, or a relative of theirs might have done an amazing thing.

These are all staple stories for a local newspaper or lifestyle magazine.

Have a go at writing a feature, telling the story of that person's life and weaving in the occasional quote.

Submit the article and telephone the editor later on to ask if it is suitable. The piece may end up being rewritten by one of the journalists but it will be a useful lesson for you to compare your efforts with the polished, professional article which is eventually published. Practice makes perfect, like many other things in life.

If you don't feel confident about writing the piece, make sure you get all the details down after talking to the individual. Take a photograph as well and send the material in to the publication with contact details for yourself.

Journalists are always grateful for useful content. They will write the feature themselves and they may even give you a byline as a reward for your hard work in uncovering the story in the first place.

3 Write a sports match report

If you play for a local football, cricket or hockey team, for example, why not write a report on your latest match.

Have a look at the way the newspaper covers sport and try to write your article in the same style.

Less is more with sports writing. Most submitted match reports are much too long and they end up frustrating the poor sports editor who must re-write it, often cutting out three-quarters of the content.

So stick to the facts. The final score, the team line-ups, the chronological order of the scoring and the context of the game – whether it is a league or cup fixture or a friendly – are all important components.

If the outcome of the game swung on a particular incident then start with that in your introduction and explain what the implications were for both teams.

Try to get someone to take line-up pictures of both teams if you are involved in actually playing and submit those as well.

A good proportion of the stories and match reports you see on the sports pages of a local paper have been submitted by players, managers or spectators.

So don't be afraid to send one in yourself, particularly if you want to be a sports writer but even if your aspirations are on the news desk.

This chapter showed you what you need to do to make an impression on the journalism industry and to show editors and other senior journalists that you have what it takes to make a career in the trade.

Next, I will assume you have been good enough to be granted an interview for a trainee journalism position with a newspaper or a broadcaster and I will give you some great advice on how you can come across really positively and get that dream job.

CHAPTER 10

HOW TO DO A GREAT INTERVIEW FOR A TRAINEE JOURNALIST JOB

CHAPTER 10: How to do a great interview for a trainee journalist job

I can't promise you will get a job as a trainee journalist but if you follow the interview advice in this chapter there will have to be a very good candidate who gets it ahead of you.

As we discussed in Chapter 9, you need to have undertaken at least a week's work experience, preferably at a local weekly or regional newspaper.

If you manage to get two placements at different news outlets then your CV will look even more impressive.

And you should arrive at your interview armed with a book of press clippings from published work in newspapers or magazines, from the reports you sent in and from your period of work experience.

Imagine if you are up against another interviewee who has a university degree in an unrelated subject but no work experience in journalism and no published articles in the media.

An editor, or whoever is interviewing you, will almost instantly value the practical expertise you have already accrued in the industry and you will already be a long way down the road to actually getting the job.

You will have detailed your work placement in your CV and also included titles where you have had work published.

TOP TIPS FOR YOUR CV

Many job adverts are over-subscribed and it is likely that trainee journalist vacancies will attract plenty of applicants.

For this reason I would advise that you send in a short concise covering letter and a one-page CV.

Editors are under-resourced in the current economic climate and they don't have the time they once had to sift through every line on a job application.

So your aim is to convince them quickly that you are a suitable candidate in as few words as possible.

a) The covering letter should simply give your address, the address of the newspaper or broadcaster where you are applying, the reference number for the job (if there is one) or job title and three or four sentences briefly explaining who you are, why you are applying and why you would be the ideal person for the role.

b) Address the letter to the relevant person at the news outlet. 'Dear sir/madam' will not suffice when you are trying to convince journalists that you can dig out stories or research an investigative piece. Check the publication or the website for the name or simply telephone them and ask before you send the application in.

c) Your CV should cover one side of an A4 piece of paper. Start with a three-line profile of yourself at the top – what you are good at, what your relevant work and study experience is and what career you are seeking.

d) Detail your work experience under another heading and explain your responsibilities in each job and how they are relevant to your application for the trainee journalist post. Include part-time roles and any voluntary or charity duties you've performed.

e) Include your educational qualifications and any other training in the next section but don't go into too much detail here – it is sufficient to mention you got a pass unless you have straight As of course!

f) Your personal details go under the next heading, date of birth, marital status and whether you have any children.

g) The final section is your personal interests. Include any sports you play or watch, hobbies you enjoy or unusual achievements. If you write novels in your spare time, for example, or you ran the London Marathon for charity then these are interesting insights into your personality for the interviewer.

10 classic interview questions for a trainee journalist job (and how to answer them)

So you have got an interview as a trainee journalist but how do you take that next giant step and impress your interviewers enough to be taken on?

If you do nothing else make sure you have read the newspaper or magazine you are hoping to work for or you have listened to news bulletins on the broadcast channel where the vacancy is.

It's not enough to have read the most recent issue, you should aim to look at a selection of copies going back probably 12 months.

I can't stress this strongly enough. If you've not read the title or familiarised yourself with its content you won't get the job. It's that simple.

You will likely be interviewed by at least two people, the editor and another senior journalist.

It goes without saying that you should be there in good time, giving yourself a moment to relax and think about what you are going to say, and dressed smartly.

Many newsrooms no longer insist on ties but you want to make a good impression so wear smart trousers, a formal shirt, a blazer or jacket and a tie if you are a man and similarly smart and professional dress if you are a woman.

I have sat in on a number of job interviews, many for people who are new to the industry, and these are the common questions you will almost certainly face at your interview.

Q1: Tell me about yourself?

This is your chance to make a good early impression. Describe your personal qualities, your education and your interests and hobbies.

Remember, they are looking for someone who will fit well into a small, dynamic team and if you come across well it is a great start to the interview.

This question is all about you as a person rather than your passion for journalism and your writing experience.

Q2: Why have you applied for this job?

Here is where you make your first pitch for the post. There will have been a job description available with the advert and you will have needed to read carefully through it.

Dissect the job description line by line and make a note of where you have the skills and the experience to effectively perform the role.

Make sure you get across your passion for becoming a journalist and mention anyone who has inspired you. Perhaps mention a reporter at the publication who impressed you with his or her reports on a particular issue.

Q3: Have you had any work experience in journalism?

This is where you mention your work experience. And if you have two separate work placements to talk about then so much the better.

Of course, it might be the case that you have already worked at the title where the vacancy is and in this case describe what you got from the placement and how it fired your enthusiasm even further to have a career in the industry.

You can also show them your press clippings at this point and pick out a couple of them to point out how you got the story and what things you did well to get it.

Q4: Why should we employ you?

Don't hold back when you are asked this one. Highlight your commitment to the job as demonstrated by your work experience placements and your substantial clippings book.

Emphasise again why you want the job and the particular skills you have which will make you the ideal candidate.

Tell the interviewers about any knowledge you have about specific issues and organisations in the locality which will be of use to the news desk.

If you are a keen social networker then explain how you would be able to build contacts and maximise online coverage of stories by using platforms such as Twitter and Facebook.

And do flag up any prowess you might have as a photographer so you can get across that you have good multi-media skills.

Q5: What do you like about our newspaper/magazine/ radio or TV station?

The answer to this will be informed by the research you carried out on the publication or broadcaster before the interview.

The journalists who are quizzing you will be keen to see exactly how much you know about the product they put out.

It's a great idea here to pick out one or two regular items you enjoy in the publication, even if you have only started reading them after you got invited for interview.

You might also pick out a recent campaign they ran, such as a charity fundraiser or a quest to get readers to sign a petition in protest against local cuts.

Everyone has a little vanity streak in them and they will be pleased to hear any complimentary comments about their work.

Q6: Which newspapers and magazines do you read?

Be honest here. If you don't read a quality newspaper regularly then don't say you do in a bid to impress the interviewers.

If you don't buy a daily newspaper or a local one there is a fair chance you read articles online which have been shared via social media.

It's worth mentioning in this case the range of titles you see regularly and pick out a couple of publications where you enjoy the writing and explain what you like about their reporting style.

They will look for an interest in local issues so you should say that you regularly read the local paper or, if you are living at home, your parents buy a copy every week.

Don't be afraid to mention a magazine you regularly read, even if it is on an unusual topic. The interviewers recognise that everyone has a personal life and it will show another side to your personality.

Q7: Is there a future for newspapers in the digital age and, if so, why?

You will be aware that the proliferation of online news sites coupled with the significant drop in print advertising revenue has dramatically hit sales of newspapers throughout the world.

It is important here to show that you think there is a future for newspapers, both as a printed entity as well as on the internet.

Mention older relatives and other people you know who still like the feel of a physical newspaper and the generation who are not tech-savvy and who don't access online reports.

But make sure you show how vital a newspaper's website is now towards continuing to make them a viable enterprise in the 21st century.

Throw in some comments here about how weekly newspapers and local broadcasters must now step up to the challenge of providing a 24/7 news operation as daily newspapers and national radio and television channels have always done.

And how this excites you as someone new to the industry.

Q8: Tell us something happening in your life which would make a good news story?

I've seen this question asked a couple of times and on both occasions it completely threw the interviewee.

It was asked to gauge the candidate's aptitude for spotting a story.

So, just in case you get asked this or something similar, think beforehand about recent incidents in your life which a journalist would be interested in reporting on.

It might be a sports match a relative was involved in, your grandparents' golden wedding or a friend meeting a celebrity.

Demonstrate that you recognise what makes a story and it will be another big tick in the box on your job application checklist.

Q9: You will often have to do extra hours at unsociable times. How do you feel about that?

This is your opportunity to show the dedication you will have to the job if they take you on.

Explain that you are aware that there will frequently be night jobs, early starts or a requirement to work through your lunch hour.

Emphasise that you thrive on hard work and that you will be keen to report the news whenever it happens.

You might point out instances in the past where you have worked unsociable hours, as a member of bar staff, a part-time delivery job or some other work related pursuit.

Say you will pull your weight as a team player to ensure the best possible news product is published every time.

It's not a good move at this point to ask if there is time off in lieu for working extra hours, by the way. That is best explored if you are offered the post.

Q10: Do you have any questions for us?

The big temptation here is that it is clearly nearing the end of your interview and you want to relax after answering a string of testing questions.

Make sure you have a list of questions for the interviewers. If you do it will reinforce how much you want the job because you would be seen to be already imagining yourself in the role.

It's a fair chance you won't know what the salary is for the job at this stage. Most job adverts will only reveal it is a 'competitive salary', which could indicate a range of pay packets.

I would advise that you ask this right at the end of the interview. It won't count against you because the interviewers know you have bills to pay however much passion you have for the job.

You could ask the basic hours of the job, what responsibilities you will have in the early weeks of the job, what on-the-job training is provided, what equipment the journalists are given to do the job, whether there is on-site parking.

Don't go overboard with the questions – remember there will probably be between three and five candidates and it is a long process for the interviewers – but make sure you find out what you need to know.

An interview is a two-way process and the editor and his colleague are well aware that you need to know about all aspects of what would be a new career for you.

Some of you will have secured that sought-after job in journalism by using the tips in this chapter and the preceding sections to impress at interview.

Others will have soaked up the information and advice in this book to help them decide that they are very much suited to a career in the industry.

And they might be considering studying the job in more depth at college or university.

This next chapter will give you the options you have to train as a journalist, whether you want a degree or a professional qualification through the National Council for the Training of Journalists (NCTJ) or a media company's in-house scheme.

CHAPTER 11

TRAINING COURSES, JOURNALISM DEGREES AND ESSENTIAL RESOURCES

CHAPTER 11: Training courses, journalism degrees and essential resources

If you have you have read this far you must now be thinking seriously about a career in journalism, hopefully after being inspired by the preceding chapters.

You could be considering a short fast track training route through further education or perhaps a longer programme in higher education.

Or perhaps you want to try your luck landing a trainee position with a newspaper or broadcaster.

The following is a list of key organisations you will find useful in the next step you make in the profession.

It is not a comprehensive list but these are all important bodies and respected centres of study within the industry.

KEY ORGANISATIONS:

National Council for the Training of Journalists (NCTJ)

73 per cent of qualified UK journalists have been trained by the NCTJ so it is a good idea to seek a training course accredited by the organisation if you go down that route.

Telephone: 01799 544014

Email: info@nctj.com

Website: www.nctj.com

Broadcast Journalism Training Council (BJTC)

This organisation works in partnership with all the major broadcast companies, including the BBC, Sky News, Channel 4 News and ITN, to accredit journalism courses.

Telephone: 0845 6008789

Website: www.bjtc.org.uk

National Union of Journalists (NUJ)

This is the union for journalists and journalism and represents a broad range of media professionals to improve pay and conditions, as well as protecting and promoting media freedom, professionalism and ethical standards.

Telephone: 0207 8433700 (head office)

Email: info@nuj.org.uk

Website: www.nuj.org.uk

USEFUL RESOURCES:

The following are great sources for latest industry news and job vacancies for novice, trainee and qualified journalists.

Hold The Front Page

www.holdthefrontpage.co.uk

Press Gazette

www.pressgazette.co.uk

The Guardian

www.theguardian.com/uk/media

BBC Journalism Academy

www.bbc.co.uk/academy/journalism

FURTHER EDUCATION COURSES:

The following colleges offer fast-track training courses for graduates and people who have some experience of working in journalism.

City of Liverpool College - www.liv-coll.ac.uk

Harlow College - www.harlow-college.ac.uk

Highbury College, Portsmouth - www.highbury.ac.uk

Lambeth College, London - www.lambethcollege.ac.uk

The Sheffield College - www.sheffcol.ac.uk

UNDERGRADUATE DEGREES:

These universities offer a range of degree courses, mainly BA (Hons) qualifications.

Bournemouth University (multimedia journalism) – www.bournemouth.ac.uk

Brunel University, London - www.brunel.ac.uk

De Montfort University, Leicester - www.dmu.ac.uk

Falmouth University - www.falmouth.ac.uk

Glasgow Caledonian University (multimedia journalism) – www.gcu.ac.uk

Glyndwr University, North Wales (certificate in higher education) – www.glyndwr.ac.uk

Leeds Trinity University - www.leedstrinity.ac.uk

Nottingham Trent University - www.ntu.ac.uk

Staffordshire University, Stoke-on-Trent - www.staffs.ac.uk

Teeside University, Middlesbrough (sports journalism) - www.tees.ac.uk

University of Brighton (travel journalism) - www.brighton.ac.uk

University of Central Lancashire, Preston - www.uclan.ac.uk

University of Essex (multimedia journalism) - www.essex.ac.uk

University of Kent (journalism & the news industry) - www.kent.ac.uk

University of Lincoln - www.lincoln.ac.uk

University of Portsmouth - www.port.ac.uk

University of Sheffield - www.sheffield.ac.uk

University of Sunderland - www.sunderland.ac.uk

POSTGRADUATE DEGREES:

If you've taken a degree in another subject and you want to become a journalist then these courses would be ideal for you. Many of the universities listed also offer undergraduate degrees as you will already have seen in this section so I won't repeat the website addresses of those.

Brunel University

Cardiff University - www.cardiff.ac.uk

De Montfort University, Leicester

Glasgow Caledonian University

Kingston University - www.kingston.ac.uk

Leeds Trinity University

Nottingham Trent University

St Mary's University, Twickenham - www.stmarys.ac.uk

Staffordshire University

Teeside University

Ulster University, Northern Ireland - www.ulster.ac.uk

University of Central Lancashire

University of Kent, Chatham - www.kent.ac.uk

University of Salford - www.salford.ac.uk

University of Sheffield

University of Sunderland

University of Sussex, Brighton - www.sussex.ac.uk

PHOTOJOURNALISM COURSES:

These are mainly three-year BA (Hons) courses. There are, of course, dedicated courses for specialist press photographers but this book is aimed at helping multi-media journalists who are able to write and take press photographs.

London College of Communication - www.arts.ac.uk/lcc

Staffordshire University

University of South Wales - www.southwales.ac.uk

University of Gloucestershire - www.glos.ac.uk

University of Wales - www.wales.ac.uk

Kingston University, London

BROADCAST JOURNALISM DEGREES:

University of the West of Scotland - www.uws.ac.uk

Cardiff University

University of Bedfordshire - www.beds.ac.uk

Leeds Trinity University

Nottingham Trent University

Birmingham City University - www.bcu.ac.uk

University of Central Lancashire

City University London - www.city.ac.uk

<u>NEWSPAPER COMPANIES (LOCAL AND REGIONAL PRESS):</u>

There are opportunities to train or complete your training on publications run by these companies.

Johnston Press

Owns 13 paid-for daily papers, 195 paid-for weeklies, 40 free titles, 10 lifestyle magazines and 198 local news and e-commerce websites.

www.johnstonpress.co.uk

Newsquest

Owns more than 200 newspapers, magazines and trade publications, including 19 daily papers.

www.newsquest.co.uk

Trinity Mirror

Owns five national newspapers and more than 100 regional newspapers.

www.trinitymirror.com

Archant

Owns more than 50 regional newspapers and is the UK's largest publisher of regional and local lifestyle magazines.

www.archant.co.uk

Press Association

A national news agency for the UK and Ireland.

www.pressassociation.com/Training

WHAT'S NEXT FOR YOU?

If you've read every chapter in this book and you've done my practical exercises for writing stories and features you will be feeling a lot more confident about going to work in a newsroom, whether it is a newspaper, a radio station or a television channel.

I've written the book to help those of you who are considering journalism as a career, students who are already studying the profession and for adults thinking about making a career change.

Hopefully I've conveyed some of the passion I have for the industry from working in newspapers for more than 20 years.

I'm really keen to help the next generation of journalists so if you have any questions which aren't answered in this book then feel free to email me at nrennie157@gmail.com and I will pass on my knowledge and advice. I also run a number of bespoke journalism training courses, which will be perfect if you are serious about getting into this profession. You can find out more here:

www.JournalismCourses.co.uk

If you are on Twitter you can also Tweet me on my page @renster157 and I would be delighted to connect with you on LinkedIn at uk.linkedin.com/in/NickRennie1 where I often post developments within the journalism industry and links to relevant blogs.

If you feel you require more guidance to prepare you for a career in journalism then take a look at the one-day training courses I run by going online to www.journalism-courses.co.uk .

These are small training groups in various UK locations where I will go into more depth on some of the content featured in the book.

There will be practical exercises on writing news and features and I will show you how you can set yourself up as a journalist on the various social media channels.

You will also have the opportunity to ask me for advice on your own career and I can help you get that vital first step in the door at a newspaper or broadcaster or help you develop your skills if you have already begun a trainee job or a professional or academic course in the subject.

I am also available for one-to-one coaching if you feel you require a more personal development programme. In this instance I can mentor you by helping you gain work experience in the industry and to create a portfolio of press work which will help you secure a trainee position. We can also work on your writing skills to help you turn out fantastic stories and features every time you sit at your keyboard.

For more details on this package please email me at nrennie157@gmail. com for further information.

Additionally, I would be willing to speak in schools or universities to help students find out more about a career in journalism.

So feel free to pass on my email address to teachers or lecturers if you would like me to give a presentation on how to become a journalist.

Finally, I would like to wish all of my readers the best of luck in their quest for a career in the profession.

I have never regretted becoming a journalist and if this book has convinced a few more people to do so then I will be very happy indeed.

Best wishes,

Nick Rennie

www.JournalismCourses.co.uk

FREQUENTLY ASKED QUESTIONS

I am pretty certain I have covered everything you need to know about how to become a journalist.

But, just in case I missed something out I would like to end with a section answering some of the most common questions I get asked by budding journalists and people who are just fascinated by the profession.

Q1 Do I need professional or academic qualifications to become a journalist?

- There is no definitive answer to this. If you get some good work experience and build a portfolio of press cuttings you can get a trainee position with no formal training behind you. There may well be some form of in-house training or a block release NCTJ course arranged for you after you have been there for a period of time. Obviously, if you take an NCTJ-backed journalism course or a degree in the subject it will increase your chances of getting into the profession. Of course, if you follow all the advice in this book it can also provide a short cut for you into the industry!

Q2 If I want a career change from journalism at some point are there any professions I can transfer my skills to?

- Many journalists end up moving into public relations because digital PR requires good writers and people who can communicate effectively with the media. Most companies and organisations also have press officers who work to raise their profile in the media with press releases and features. The writing is different because it is purely promotional as opposed to the neutral, balanced articles news outlets produce.

Q3 I am dyslexic. Does that mean I have no chance of becoming a journalist?

- In the past dyslexia may have been a serious drawback for a budding journalist. Spelling words correctly and using good English grammar has always been vital and modern technology allows us to do a spell check before we file our stories. There will also be a sub-editor and a proof-reader who will check what you've written if you work for a print media outlet. In fact, some very good journalists have overcome having dyslexia to make a successful career in the industry.

Q4 I want to work in a television or radio newsroom so should I aim to get work experience in those industries rather than newspapers?

- By all means try to get a work placement with a broadcaster to see how it all works. You may not get any 'on air' experience, though, whereas a newspaper will allow you to write stories. Many of our top radio and television reporters started out on newspapers. Local or regional newspapers will give you a solid grounding in journalism and help you develop your news sense so it is well worth looking for a placement with one of them.

Q5 I keep hearing that newspapers are struggling and they have no future so is it worth trying to get into the industry?

- It's true that newspapers were slow to adapt to the digital age. Readers deserted print titles as the internet flourished and news could be accessed free on the web. Newspapers were initially understandably hesitant about putting their stories on the internet for free, particularly at a time when advertising revenues were dipping. But the industry is now embracing online publishing and the increased web traffic allows them to charge more for advertising on the internet. Newspapers will survive and flourish in my opinion, although more readers are likely to access them via tablet computers or their PCs rather than printed issues in years to come.

Q6 I've never been tech-savvy. Would that hold me back in a journalism career?

- If you look at journalist job adverts on the websites of *Hold The Front Page* or the *Press Gazette*, for example, you will see many include the requirement to have good digital skills. Today's reporters have to be multi-media journalists, able to take a good photograph or record a video interview as well as take a shorthand note when they are out on an assignment. It's essential you practice on cameras and camcorders and that you are able to process the images and films for use in your news organisation. As we discussed earlier in the book, a working understanding of social media is also important.

Q7 I want to work on a national newspaper so is there any point in me working on a small local weekly?

- It is very difficult to get a trainee position on one of the nationals although some exceptional individuals do manage to do it. It's worth remembering that many high profile journalists started out on a local weekly, including Michael Parkinson, Piers Morgan, Angela Rippon, Richard Madeley and Jeremy Clarkson. The same is true of top reporters working on national radio and television – many of them started off working for small, regional broadcasters. You learn so many of the important principles working in the local media and there is plenty of time to graduate to the bright lights of the *Sunday Times* or the *BBC* newsroom.

Q8 What sort of wage can I expect to get as a trainee?

- This can vary, of course, depending whether you begin on a local newspaper or broadcaster or one of the national media outlets. Your starting salary is likely to be between £15,000 and £22,000 per year, although you will be able to increase that considerably when you qualify as a senior, either through an in-house training scheme or an NCTJ-accredited programme. The higher you go in the profession the more you will be rewarded for your talents. Your pay packet will be into six figures if you can graduate to a prominent role with a national newspaper, magazine or broadcaster.

Q9 How do I get into a specialist journalism area like sports writing, court reporting or movie reporting?

- Once again you are best advised to start at a small weekly or regional newspaper or a local radio or television station. You need to learn the ropes and you will get the perfect grounding at a lower profile media outlet. You will get the opportunity to try your hand at a wider range of journalistic disciplines and get the experience you need to become proficient. News writing is a great grounding for sports writing because you will develop a great news sense and principles which will help you produce top sports copy when you get the chance. The same is true of any specialism – my advice is to get some experience on the news desk and then think about making the move into a specific discipline.

Q10 What kind of promotion prospects do I have after I have completed my training?

- Today's young reporters quickly become multi-media journalists because they need to be able to write great copy for print and online, as well as take good quality photographs and shoot video footage for a website. Because of this I believe journalists develop much quicker than when I started out, when there were more people working with you and opportunities to shadow colleagues and learn at your own pace. Young journalists feeding today's rolling 24/7 news agenda quickly become important members of staff and as such they get the chance to advance their careers far quicker than even five years ago. It is true that there are fewer people working in print and broadcast news outlets but there are huge opportunities to climb the career ladder if you are good enough.

Q11 How do I become a radio or television news reporter?

- There are fewer broadcasters than newspapers so it follows that there are fewer opportunities to get into radio or television with little experience behind you. If radio is something you have set your heart on then it is worth getting experience running your own hospital radio show or seeking work with the university station if you are still studying. If television reporting is more your thing you should practice giving reports in front of a camcorder and perhaps think about setting up your own You Tube news reporting channel. If you do it well enough it will be a great addition to your CV. And, of course, you should apply for traineeships on local newspapers to give you that all-important grounding in news and how you should report it. It will help you make a move into broadcasting when the opportunity arises.

Q12 What are the pros of being a journalist?

- One of the best things about the job is that every day is different, particularly when you are a reporter. You might be interviewing a school head teacher about a new dining hall one minute and then chatting to a pensioner who has just completed a parachute jump for charity. Other times you could be in court following a murder trial or rubbing shoulders with a celebrity at a business launch event or awards night. You will get to meet so many different people through the job. Some of them will annoy you intensely, others will move and inspire you. And you get to reveal important news often before anyone else has heard about it. That is the real buzz of being a journalist, no matter what level of the profession you work in.

Q13 Are there any downsides to the job?

- Not every assignment is glamorous. Sometimes you will be tasked to source stories at a late night council meeting and occasionally you will have to cancel your evening plans to work on a breaking story. I guarantee you will put in more hours than you are paid for but then that is the nature of the job – you need to be driven to find out the news even if it requires you to go through a longer working day to do so. You will have to bite your lip on occasions, when someone is unfairly criticising your media organisation at a public meeting, for example, or when a telephone caller is demanding you report on their inconsequential news item. But the pros certainly outweigh the cons when it comes to following a career in journalism.

Q14 I have a criminal record. Can I still become a journalist?

- You most certainly can but it might depend on the offence you have committed. What I would say is that you should not try to hide your conviction when you apply for work to a newspaper or broadcaster. That would most definitely go against you if you are found to be fabricating your CV. Providing the offence was not too serious you should still be able to find work as a journalist. In some cases your experiences of breaking the law may even land you a specialist reporting job. In fact, the Guardian's prison correspondent is someone who has spent many years of his life in jail and his background makes him the ideal person to write about the prison service in this country.

Q15 Realistically, what salary can I expect to receive as a journalist once I have a decent level of experience under my belt?

- If you are working for a local or regional newspaper you would expect to earn around £25,000 when you have five years of experience behind you. As you climb up the career ladder to a senior editorial post your annual wage should be around £40,000. If you progress to a job with a national newspaper you will significantly increase your income, particularly if you become a specialist correspondent or a senior editor where wages of £70,000 and much more will be paid. If you are working as a freelance you would be charging between £120 and £150 for a day's work as a reporter or sub-editor on a local weekly or daily and up to £180 on a national.

Experienced broadcast journalists can earn between £21,000 and £45,000 with the top national reporters receiving pay packets of more than £80,000.

Q16 Are there any fast track routes into journalism?

- If you shine on a work placement at a newspaper or broadcaster then other members of staff will notice. This means bringing stories in or contributing good story ideas at a news conference. The way you interact with other people while on work experience also influences the way others assess your qualities, whether that is interviewing someone for a report or asking intelligent questions of a reporter or editor. Basically, your best chance of getting a fast track into journalism is how you perform on your work placements. If you are good and a news organisation has a trainee opening then they will snap you up. Reading this book, of course, will also give you a huge advantage when it comes to making a career in journalism.

Q17 I can be a little sensitive in certain situations. Does that mean I won't be tough enough to become a good reporter?

- Showing empathy towards other people is an important quality in a journalist. You have to be compassionate when you are interviewing the relatives of someone who has died suddenly, for example, or if you are talking to the parents of a child who is seriously ill. So being sensitive is not a major issue in this line of work. There may be occasions when you have to report on a tragic incident or you come into contact with aggressive and abusive individuals. But if you are cut out for a career in the industry then your journalistic qualities will come to the fore to help you get the story you are pursuing.

Q18 I am quite interested in becoming a freelance journalist. Are there many opportunities to do that?

- More media organisations are using freelance journalists than ever before. I have worked for local and regional newspapers in this way for the last three years and there is plenty of work available. It's also a good way of earning money when you are studying journalism or preparing yourself to apply for a trainee post. If your work is good enough, a newspaper or broadcaster will pay you for it. Following the basic principles I have set out in this book will give you a good grounding even if you have never worked in a newsroom. Gaining practical experience of what it is like to be a journalist will help you develop your skills further and all the better if you are paid while you are doing it. Once you have trained, completed your studies or worked in the media for a few years you will then have endless opportunities to freelance in various areas of the industry.

Q19 What are the advantages of being a freelance compared to being employed as a full-time journalist attached to just one media organisation?

- The obvious advantage of freelancers is the way you can pick and choose who you work for. You can work at two or three news outlets in the same week and work with different people in different surroundings. And that can be inspiring and motivating. If you don't enjoy working with a particular employer you can go and work somewhere else at the drop of a hat. Freelancers can claim business expenses for things like buying a laptop or a camera, mobile phone bills, stationary and car costs, to reduce their tax bill. You also have total flexibility about when you work and when you take your holidays. The big negative for freelancers is the lack of security. You have no working contract so an employer can decide not to use you again for whatever reason and that could be with immediate effect. Additionally, you won't get paid when you take a holiday or a break from work or when you are off sick.

Q20 Are there any newspapers you would recommend I should read or broadcasters I should listen to and watch to get an insight into the world of journalism?

- Anyone interested in becoming a journalist should read a newspaper, listen to the news on the radio and watch the TV news bulletins simply because you need to be aware of current affairs and topical items. Read the tabloids like the *Sun* or the *Mirror* as well as scanning copies of the quality dailies like *The Times* and the *Guardian* and the mid-range titles such as the *Daily Mail*. But also read your local papers, especially if you are looking for a route into the industry through a trainee position or an internship. Get yourself up-to-date with the issues which affect your community and you will be in a great position when an opening arises. It's very much the same situation with the broadcasters, if that is where you are setting your sights. Listen to the local radio station as well as *BBC Radio 4's* Today programme or *BBC 5 Live's* Drive show and watch your regional television news bulletin as well as the *Channel 4 News* or *Sky News* output. Great journalism is all around you and it would be a waste if you didn't soak it all up in your quest for a career in the profession.